Building Your Dream Barndominium

The Complete Guide To Getting Your Barn Home Built From The Ground Up

Maddie Cohen

By reading this document, the reader agrees that under no circumstances is the author responsible for any losses, direct or indirect, that are incurred as a result of the use of the information contained within this document, including, but not limited to, errors, omissions, or inaccuracies.

TABLE OF CONTENTS

Introduction

The thought of living in a barn doesn't appeal to everyone. In fact, not so long-ago barns were only enticing to the animals that lived in them. How times have changed! If you've ever heard the word 'barndominium' then you know that living in a barn is no longer frowned upon. For my family and I, not just living in, but actually building our very own barn-style home had been a dream for an exceptionally long time. I think I can easily trace my love of the barndominium concept back to working on household projects with my dad. As my love for architecture and design grew, so did my desire to build my own barn-type home. Fortunately, it wasn't difficult to convince my husband, four children and three adorable golden retrievers that the barn lifestyle was meant for us.

Opting to embrace the barndominium dream didn't come without its hiccups or sacrifices. Despite my extensive background in design and architecture, my husband and I were still met with many challenges as we set out to make our dream of building our first barndominium a reality. We are after all, what we like to refer to as, *barndo dreamers*. If you've given the barndominium lifestyle more than a passing thought, you may be at risk of being a barndo dreamer too.

Essentially, people dream of building their own barndominiums for three reasons. The first has to do with space. If you have four kids in a three-bedroom city house and a menagerie of pets, then you'll understand the dilemma with space. Trying to keep a family happy and off each other's nerves can be quite a mission when they're of varying ages and continuously in each other's space. A large family in a small space always feels like no one has any privacy and everything always ends up looking cluttered. Add to that the possibility of trying to run a business out of that space, and you may just have an instant recipe for madness.

The second reason you might be attracted to building your own barndominium has to do with wanting your own unique living space. Living in a cookie-cutter city house or apartment can be somewhat stifling after a while. After all, how exciting and unique can you make a home that looks pretty much like the next one? Change the drapes? Paint the fence? If you're reading this book, and you live in one of those carbon-copy city homes, then you know exactly what we're talking about.

Thirdly, people often consider the barndominium concept because it's the ideal way to combine your business and your residential space. Depending on the type of business you run, having it next door to your home can have several benefits. No commute, close to your family and of course you can adjust your working hours without neglecting your family. With the extensive floor plan options, you can create anything from a small bead business to a medium-sized winery in your barndo.

Does reading this make you want to shout out a resounding, "Yeah, I get you?" If you're experiencing one or all of these irritations, building a barndominium might just be the solution you need. We had our barndominium dream for a long time before we were able to make it a reality. Despite knowing what we wanted and what to expect, the final results were (and still are) astounding.

In short, we traded our cramped city house for an open floorplan home with more than double the space we previously had. No more clutter, and no more family members getting on each other's nerves because of a lack of space. Moreover, we were able to build our barndominium in Texas, where we could (and still do) enjoy a bunch of fun outdoor activities. Additionally, our three golden retrievers have never had so much room to run around.

With that said, you too can build your own barndominium. We're not here to tell you that it's going to happen from one day to the next. But, we (my husband and I, that is) do want you to know that having your own barndominium may be more achievable than you think. If you've already decided that you're going to build your own barn-style home, you may be a bit bewildered over where to start the process. We've been in your shoes. Many times we wished we had a simple, straightforward guide that combines different tips and hacks to simplify the behind-the-scenes processes.

As we've already mentioned, we had our fair share of ups and downs when we started our project. Sometimes running from pillar to post, which resulted in what seemed like ages of delays. With that in mind, we decided to write this book, which is essentially just a basic guide to the barndominium-building process. In short, you're going to learn how to start the barndominium dream from the very beginning. How to find the right location and how to approach potential lenders are just two of the important aspects we'll share.

If you're wondering what qualifies us to write this book, the answer is simple. ***We've lived the journey.*** Aside from an extensive background in design, architecture and building projects, we also endured each step of the process personally. After building our first barndominium, we decided it would be an excellent idea to guide fellow barndo dreamers through the basic process of building their dream barndo.

Our comprehensive guide isn't a step-by-step contractor's handbook on how to lay foundations or hang the drywall. What it is though, is a few crucial tips and tricks to help you along each step of the process. We like to believe that we're sharing valuable information that will save you hours of back and forth.

We hope you enjoy this book and find our tips and guidelines instrumental in getting your barndominium built with as little stress as possible. Keep reading as we start our guide by sharing a few good reasons why everyone should be living in a barndominium!

Chapter 1: Why a Barndominium?

Our first thought when asked this question is actually, "Why not?" Since not everyone shares our passion for the barndo lifestyle, it sometimes takes some convincing. Which, we don't mind, since we believe everyone should be living in a barndominium.

As we mentioned in our introduction, we are huge fans of the entire barndominium concept. We love the space, open plans and uniqueness of it. Whether you need a considerably larger space for your usual living area, or you want to have your business attached to your home, the barndominium concept allows for it without creating a cluttered chaotic scenario. But, before we get to a few of the fun uses for your dream barndominium, let us start at the very beginning.

What Exactly Is a Barndominium?

If you're reading this book, you most likely know exactly what a barndominium is. In fact, we're going to bet that you're as excited at the thought of living in one as we were when we first started! But, since we're sticklers for clarity, and since there are some misconceptions, we're going to clarify exactly what a barndominium is.

As the name suggests, a barndominium is essentially a barn that has been converted into an extensively large living space. Barndominiums, or barndos as they're commonly called, can be newly built based on a customized design or they can be refurbished from an existing barn. (Yes, the kind your farm animals might originally have been living in!) The goal is to use the space as a home, business or any other usable living area.

For the most part, barndominiums are large rectangular-shaped spaces boasting open-living concepts. This type of architecture provides homeowners with an array of customizable floor plans and styles. We often refer to this as the customizable factor. Depending on what you want to do with your barndo, the customizable factor may or may not be a big deal.

To us, it was a huge deal. We wanted to create a space that was not only unique to our style but also our space requirements. We enjoyed that we could customize just about every aspect of our barndominium.

That said, barndominiums can be built from the ground up, or by using a pre-designed and prefabricated kit. Many barndo kits—as they're called—do allow for a certain amount of customization. Essentially, it's all up to you and the type of home you want to create.

Different Usages of Modern Barndominiums

There's no denying it. Living in the city, between other homes, on your specifically allocated lot, has its limits. Not only are you bound by space restrictions, but also zoning and building regulations.

One of the biggest draw cards to the barndo concept is the wide range of possibilities that are open to homeowners. A few of the most common uses that make barndos so popular are discussed below.

Create Your Family Home

If you're looking for a spacious, open-plan home with a romantic yet functional feel, then a barndominium is definitely for you. Since barndos are so spacious, they're ideal for homeowners who want more than the average three or four-bedroom home.

In fact, we've seen some floor plans with options for five, six, seven or even eight bedrooms. This depends on the size of your barndo, what else you want to use it for and, of course, the size you'd like each room to be.

Multi-Family Homes

Perhaps you've been in a situation where family is coming over for the holidays. One or two of the kids have to give up their bedrooms for the relatives to stay in during their visit. This leaves you with moody kids and cluttered spaces. Or you'd like to provide a space for your elderly parents or parents-in-law to live permanently, but you just don't have the space. There are a ton of reasons why a bigger home would be an excellent idea.

Should one of your requirements or wishes be to provide relatives with a place to stay and still ensure everyone has their privacy and their space, this is the solution for you. Barndos are ideal for creating multi-family homes without your children having to give up the privacy and sanctity of their bedrooms. It's also excellent for providing each person with their own space without feeling cluttered and cramped.

A Business Space from Home

Another top attraction to the barndominium concept is that it's so much easier to run a small to medium-sized business right next to your living area. This provides many homeowners with the comfort of being close to home (and the kids) while working. You can run a home spa, IT company or even a business that requires a small workshop area without too much hassle, from the comfort of your very own barndominium.

Have you ever been to Napa Valley for a wine tour? You'll find a few barndominiums which have been converted into wineries with tasting rooms. The possibilities are as extensive as your imagination!

The Ultimate Storage Solution

Looking for a home with additional storage? You can easily convert a section of your barndo into a storage unit. Depending on your floor plan, you can structure your storage area so that it doesn't interfere with your living area. When you no longer need the storage area, simply convert it to another room, entertainment area or playroom.

Create a Space for Farm Animals or Pets

Are you the type of person who wants to live near your farm animals, such as your horses? With the size of the average barndo, you can easily separate your space to create living quarters for them. Granted, the idea of living in the same building as your farm animals might not be everyone's cup of tea, but if it appeals to you, the barndo concept makes it that much easier. This is also a great option if your dream is to own your own riding school. Other animal-type businesses such as animal clinics, dog training schools and pet grooming services are also small enough to fit into a section of your barndo.

Folks who love dogs as much as we do can create a special play area to use during rainy or snowy days when the outdoors isn't fun. It also makes it easier to add more dogs to your family, which, for some of us, is always an excellent idea. Additionally, if you're going to build your barndo on a big enough property, there's no need to take the dogs for their daily walks. With a huge property, they can easily get the exercise they need without interrupting your schedule.

Sports/Training Arena

For kids who love sports, there may even be enough space to create an indoor sports arena. With the ample space available in most barndos, it's amazingly easy to build an indoor pool or sports arena. It's also the perfect time to create that home gym that consists not only of a riding bike in the corner.

Alternatively, if a very extensive game room for the kids (or your husband) is more up your alley, the good news is that it's a lot more possible than it would be in a conventional-sized home in the city. Creating a large game and entertainment room is also an excellent way to keep children occupied when miserable winter weather limits outdoor fun.

Greenhouse

We have also recently seen a friend turn a large chunk of their barndominium into a greenhouse. That way they get to nurture their garden or grow their food even in the colder months when snow or harsh temperatures prevail. Moreover, it's a perfect way to create your own organic garden to improve the quality of the food you're consuming. Since most barndos are built in rural areas, having a greenhouse is a perfect opportunity to get involved with a local farmer's market. Joining the local market is a great way to earn some extra cash, even if starting a business wasn't your main goal.

Income Generator

Another option to consider is using your free barndominium space as an income generator. Create a few smaller living areas that can be rented out to bring in additional outcomes. Of course, here your location would play a huge factor in order for this to work successfully. Depending on the size of your barndo, you may even consider turning a small space into a B&B or even Airbnb.

The Pros and Cons of It All

As with other types of building structures, barndos have a wide range of pros and cons. And, as any homeowner who has ever built their own home will tell you, diving into such a huge financial commitment requires due consideration of all the pros and cons. Here's a list of all the pros and cons that we considered when we were planning our beautiful barndo.

Pros

Budget-Friendly: The top advantage of a barndo is its cost-effective building and general maintenance costs. Most times, a barndo is much cheaper than a conventional home of a similar size. This has to do with the need for fewer walls in a barndo.

- **Pet-Friendly:** Living in an apartment or city home often restricts the number of pets you can have. Try having three golden retrievers in a small city home! Living in a bando allows you to give your pets (and other animals) adequate space.

- **Highly Customizable**: Since barndos are very customizable, they can be designed and adapted to suit each homeowner's unique style and needs. Design styles can vary from classic wooden farmhouse structures to uber-modern metal frames. Some barndos are a combination of wood and steel—it all depends on the homeowner's decor style.

- **Comfort:** For people who want to enjoy the comfort of space, the barndo concept is a godsend. Say goodbye to cramped, cluttered living spaces! We should mention that this option works extremely well with large families as it offers everyone their own space without getting in each other's personal space. It also enables you to arrange your furniture spaciously without having to rearrange the whole house to have a dinner party!

- **Open Concept:** Many homeowners prefer the open-concept design style, where rooms flow into each other and there are no walls blocking spaces. Spaces can also be more easily utilized if the area isn't restricted to a specific size. It's also perfect for larger styles of furniture that require more space to blend into your decor.

- **Easy Entertainment:** Have you ever tried to entertain thirty of your closest friends and family in your conventional city home? It can become crowded quite quickly. With a barndo, you can easily create a designated entertainment area, complete with its own appliances and furniture. That way you keep guests out of your living area, and you only have one area to clean afterward. A designated area is perfect for birthdays, work functions or even kid's playdates.

- **Durability:** Despite the many design options, most homeowners opt for steel frames. This makes for a more durable structure. In fact, an article in Barndominium Life has claimed that a steel band structure can withstand an F-4 tornado.

- **Room for Growth:** For a growing family, a barndo is ideal. A bigger initial space will ensure that you have adequate room for additional bedrooms and bathrooms. In our case, it was a wonderful excuse to get a few more dogs.

- **Takes less Time to build:** On average, a barndominium takes between 3–6 months to build. Factors such as size, materials, and permits needed play a huge role in determining the time taken. It's not uncommon for smaller barndo projects to be built in a few weeks.

- **Easy to Add Stylish Features:** Adding different design elements to your barndo is also much easier. Wrap-around porches, vaulted ceilings, visible ceiling beams or trusses are just a few examples of features that can be added to your barndo to create a unique and functional space.

- **Dual-Purpose Home:** Barndominiums provide homeowners with a superior dual-purpose solution to combine living space with a business or home office.

- **Eco-Friendly:** Many American barndominium contractors opt for eco-friendly building materials. This, in turn, will help you reduce your carbon footprint, taking you a little closer to sustainable living.

- **Easy to Renovate:** With a spacious, open-plan design, it's much easier to renovate your barndo when you want to upgrade your decor style. There are no walls to knock down to create bigger spaces!

Cons

- **Corrosion:** Metal structures form the base of many modern barndominiums. Choosing a steel material puts your structure at risk of corrosion unless routinely treated.

- **Wood Rotting:** If you prefer a traditional barndo made of wood, you must factor in the potential effects of wood insects such as termites. There's also the risk of dampness in very humid areas. Opting for a wooden structure will require additional costs of specialized treatments and yearly maintenance.

- **City Restrictions:** As you continue your research, you'll soon discover that not all cities permit barndominiums. It's important to check all aspects of barndo laws in your preferred location. This concept might not be ideal for people who prefer to be close to the hustle and bustle of the city.

- **Single-Story Floor Designs:** While most barndos are single-story structures, you can opt for an additional story, but this will obviously cost more than you might have initially expected.

- **Outside Noise Transfers:** Barndo's constructed from steel or metal transfer sounds a lot easier. Rain and wind can sound incredibly loud when bashing against a steel barndo frame. While there are measures you can take to combat this, remember that this will need to be added to your budget.

- **Fire Sprinkler Systems:** Depending on the area you've chosen for your dream barndo, there may be specific building codes in place. This will dictate that you install a fire sprinkler system. Bear in mind, this won't be a one-time expense, as there'll be maintenance and compliance tests to factor into your budget.

- **Insulation:** Barndos that are going to be used solely as a living space, may require additional insulation to keep rooms warmer in the winter. Depending on the size of your barndo, this could be a costly addition. In some states, insulation is a prerequisite before moving in.
- **Pest Control:** Folks wanting to share their barndo space with animals may require additional pest control. A whole variety of unwanted pests are likely to move in when you house your horse in your living area. Pest control will need to be done routinely.
- **Difficult Financing:** Finding adequate financing for a barndo structure can be a huge hassle—we will cover this topic in extensive detail in a later chapter.

What Is the Lifespan of a Barndominium

If you've been researching the barndo concept, you've undoubtedly asked yourself how long a barndominium will last before you have to rebuild. The good news is, if your barndo is built correctly, you can easily look at a considerably longer life span.

Generally, the average barndo has a lifespan ranging between 50 and 150 years. This, of course, depends on the materials used in construction and how well the building has been maintained. Of course, the weather also plays a huge factor and how it interacts with the material. For instance, metal is more susceptible to corrosion in humid weather, while wood is at risk of insect damage and wood rot.

Our pro tip: *Opt for materials and maintenance plans that will increase the durability of your dream barndo. Speak to your general contractor about correctly treating any wooden materials you're using. Additionally, opt for quality insulation from day one.*

Do Barndominiums Hold Any Resale Value?

Most homeowners don't think of selling their property while they are building their dream homes. It may, however, be something you might consider down the line. That said, it's important to consider whether your barndo will hold any resale value.

Mostly, barndominiums hold their resale value quite well. However, it's important to mention that most barndos are created to suit an owner's specific space requirements.

Mostly, a barndos resale value will almost always exceed the initial cost of construction.

JJ's Custom Builders recently published an article in which they state that a traditional home only appreciates at a rate of about 4% per year. While there is currently no specific quantifier for barndos, their appreciations are considerably higher. This is largely due to their various customizable aspects.

With that in mind, it's always an excellent idea to add standout features to your barndo. Of course, I'm talking about the features that would impress the average barndo home hunter. Some perks that add to the resale value of your barndo include:

- Skylights
- Solar energy
- Energy-efficient windows and doors
- Balconies (for two story barndos)
- Wrap-around or enclosed porches
- Spacious rooms
- Open floor-plan designs
- Modern, water-saving plumbing fixtures
- Outdoor entertainment area

Key Takeaways

When you're reviewing your options about whether or not a barndo is for you and your family, consider the following:

- Identify what you want to do with your barndo—will it be a home or serve as a business as well?
- Consider the pros and cons of barndominium living—the good news is that there are considerably more reasons to be building your own barndo.
- As you start planning your barndo dream, assess the potential resale value and the features that will enhance the value of your dream home.

We'll discuss adding these options in more detail later on, so keep reading!

Chapter 2: Budgeting

Have you started the budgeting process for your barndominium process? This is the one aspect that will shape your barndo dream as it determines the size, add-ons and upgrades you're open to considering. That said, budgeting for a barndo is a process that requires more than just a little thought.

Many barndo builders agree that on average a barndominium construction can exceed its planned budget by between 5% and 15% of the original budget. In addition, this can get quite hectic if you add your monthly loan repayment in relation to your monthly income.

This chapter takes a look at a few important factors to consider when you're drawing up your budget. It's easy to overlook a few crucial points if this is the first barndo you're building. Drawing up our budget was one of the toughest challenges we faced and we hope our guide will ease your stress.

Establish Wants vs. Needs

Before we jump into the factors that should determine your budget, it's important to understand there's often a huge divide between what you *want* your barndo to have and look like and what it actually *needs*.

That means, sticking to what's needed will go a long way to keeping your barndo building process within budget. If you're new to the barndo building concept, it might not always be easy to distinguish your barndo *wants* from the *needs*. To give you an idea of the difference, we've listed a few hypothetical scenarios.

- Your barndo *needs* windows, but you might *want* larger bay windows bigger than standard options.
- Large, heavy-themed doors, as opposed to regular doors, is a *want*, not a *need*.
- A bigger swimming pool is a *want* rather than a *need*.

Another way to look at it is determining what you're prepared to go without in your barndo in the initial stages. There are aspects that you can add or upgrade as time goes on and more funds become available.

Be sure to draw up a list with columns for WANT, NEED and LATER. When it comes to listing items under the 'LATER' column, opt for factors that won't need the building team to come back, as this will be costly.

Estimated Cost Breakdown

Many barndo dreamers first setting out often feel frustrated that there is seldom a hard and fast upfront cost for their barndo. This is because of the highly customizable factor. The answer to most budget-related questions is often "it depends."

Getting an exact cost will require a lot of research as it will involve pricing everything from insulation to windows. That in turn will also depend on the amount you require. No matter how accurately you do this, it's very seldom that two barndos will have the same cost. So, while we can't give you exact amounts, we can give you a few general estimates. That will at the very least give you an idea of what to factor in and what average prices are.

Typical Barndominium Cost to Anticipate

On average, it costs about $124,000 to complete a barndo of 2,300 square feet. Of course, the types of additions you include can dramatically swing that amount. To give you an idea of some of the costs to consider, we've used the model published in an article from Outdoorroo detailing the average breakdown of barndo costs.

Land Preparation

Essentially, land prep refers to getting the property ready for building. In instances where you've bought a rural property, it will be necessary to remove trees or shrubs in the area where the barndo will do. Your quote here will depend on the size of the land, and the preparation that needs to be done. To save costs, try to do this task yourself.

Foundation Slab, Barndo Shell and Roof

Fortunately, if you're opting for a barndo kit, the package will include a foundation slab, barndo shell, roof and standard door and windows. Purchasing one of these kits will save you a considerable amount of money rather than having to pay for each item individually.

The price of a barndo kit depends on the size and location of your property. The barndo kit supplier also plays a part in the total cost as well as extras that may be included in the package. On average a barndo kit can cost anywhere from $20 per square foot for a DIY barndo and $140 for a high-end option. That will leave you with an average cost of $70.

Light Fittings

The types of light fittings will depend on your chosen interior style. This can be anything from bare bulbs to fancier light fixtures such as chandeliers or design-appropriate lamps. In this instance, you'd most likely spend more money on the fixtures than on the actual installation. Light fittings can really range from **$75 to $500**, so you'd have to calculate what you need.

Insulation

No matter where you're building your barndo, you should choose quality insulation. This is because insulation keeps heat or cool air from escaping out of the barndo. Using insulators such as spray foam will keep your monthly energy bills in check as you won't need an AC system to be on the whole day.

On average, spray foam costs an average of **$1 to $1.50** per foot of the board. Sticking to our average 2,300 square-foot examples will cost you between **$6,903 and $10,354** for 3" of the spray foam insulation type.

Plumbing

A prerequisite to being able to move into your completed barndo is that it must have running water. Once running water is connected, you'll be able to get the necessary Certificate of Occupancy, or CO as it's commonly called.

Once again, the exact plumbing requirements will be determined by your barndos needs. If your property is close enough to the county's main line, it might be easy enough to connect to your plumbing. In general, you'll be required to buy plumbing fixtures such as sinks, showers, bathtubs and toilets. To save money here, it's a good idea to shop for these items yourself. That way you can find bargains and cost-effective options.

When you're drawing up your plumbing needs, it's essential to take into account the household appliances that will use water. Connecting a dishwasher, water heater and washing machine might push up the costs of your plumbing requirements.

With our model of a 2,300 square foot barndo, you could be looking at a plumbing cost of about **$15,000** based on the general costs of plumbers and equipment. Since plumbing is somewhat specialized, it's not a good idea to do this part as a DIY task unless you have the necessary experience. The last thing you want is a flooded barndo two months down the line.

Electrical

Electricity is crucial because you will need it to run your lights and appliances. Adding electricity to your barndo involves wiring, installing outlets and light switches as well as having a circuit panel fully installed.

As with the plumbing, you will have to hire a professional to ensure the barndo passes all the required inspections to receive the Occupancy Certificate. On average your electrical expenditure will be around **$10,000** depending on the number of outlets and appliances you need to be installed.

Windows and Doors

Since barndos are so much taller than the average home, it's often very tempting to install larger, grander types of windows. In fact, some barndo owners often install large windows that extend up to the ceiling. This can be an expensive option.

On the other hand, experts recommend using energy-efficient windows to assist in keeping energy bills affordable. Since these types of windows keep the air from escaping, they reduce the need for constant heating or cooling systems to be on all the time.

On average, an x1 energy-efficient window (and the labor to install it) costs between **$390 to $790**. Based on this you can easily calculate the total number of windows you need. Keep in mind that your barndo can have as many as 16 windows which will put your total window cost between **$6,000 and $13,000.**

When it comes to choosing doors, you'll also greatly reduce your costs by opting for standard doors rather than elaborate large, heavy doors. If you're opting for a kit, we should highlight that the door and window spaces are designed for standard fittings. Furthermore, opting for an open-plan floor design will reduce the number of doors you require inside. Choosing a regular door will cost an average of **$100** per piece while a barn door can cost as much as **$2,500.**

Painting

Depending on the type and amount of paint you're opting for, buying your own paint is still considerably cheaper than hiring a contractor to do it. In most instances, a gallon of paint will range anywhere between **$15 to $30**. Since a simple gallon of paint can easily cover about 400 square feet, you'll be able to calculate the amount you need.

For our 2,300 square feet example, you can look at spending between **$173 and $350** to add two layers of paint if you're doing it yourself. Hiring a professional on the other hand can cost as much as **$28,000** depending on the size of your barndo.

Flooring

When it comes to flooring, many barndo owners opt to choose from a host of different floor types to prevent only having the standard concrete slab. Some of these options include the more expensive hardwood floor options. The good news is that you can get engineered wood flooring that mimics the traditional hardwood floor types.

Engineered flooring might be slightly thinner than traditional hardwood but will cost you anything from **$14,000 to $18,000**. Another option that is cheaper than hardwood and engineered flooring is laminate flooring. On average laminate can cost between **$3,00 and $11,00** per square foot. Laminate is easier to install and has a wide variety of designs and colors to choose from.

A Few Extra Costs that You Might Have/Want to Include

There can be a variety of costs that fall into the "extra cost" category. Everything from an outdoor entertainment area, gazebo, awnings above the doors and even swimming pools can be added here. It's entirely up to you. We've listed the two most common extra addition barndo dreamers often include.

Fireplace

Installing a fireplace isn't one of those items that your barndo absolutely needs. (Of course, it depends where your barndo is situated) However, it was difficult for us to imagine our barndo without the classic feel of a modern fireplace. That said, the prices of modern fireplaces depend on whether or not you'd prefer an electric or gas option. A gas fireplace may also need a professional to connect the gas line. Fireplaces can cost up to **$4,000.**

HVAC System

Essentially, HVAC refers to a heating, ventilation and air conditioning system that's made up of a furnace, air ducts, air filtration and air conditioning units. The cost here depends on the size of the system you're installing. You may opt to only install it in a small section of your living area, or the whole barndo. A bigger system can be costly as well as push your monthly energy bill up. An average-sized HVAC system can easily set you back up to **$10,000.**

Factor in the Extras

When you're setting up your barndo budget, be sure to factor in the extras that aren't essential to your barndominium. In the beginning stages of building your barndo, you may even regard some of these items as "nice to haves." Here you essentially have two choices.

The first is to factor these aspects into your budget and find a way to make them happen. Generally, this train of thought stems from wanting to get everything down at once. Your other choice is to add the extras as you go along or as money becomes available. While that may ease the strain on your budget, it'll leave you with an 'incomplete' property for several more months. You will have to decide how comfortable you are with either option.

Our personal advice is to fit as much as possible into your budget. Shop for cheaper alternatives rather than "leaving them for later." With all that needs to be done in and around your barndo, it might become overwhelming to leave a long "still-to-do" list after the building team leaves.

Some extras to include in your initial budget plans include the following:

- Swimming pool
- Outdoor area patios
- Landscaping and accessories
- Driveways and walkways
- Fences and outdoor walls
- Gazebos, awnings and outdoor blinds

Potential Hidden Costs

In our extensive barndo experience, there's one thing we're very certain of. No matter how well you plan or budget for building your dream barndo, there are always hidden costs that have a tendency of popping up at the most inopportune times. If your budget is already at its limit, these costs can really hamper the whole process. Here are some potential hidden costs that might not have been at the forefront of your mind.

- **Permit Fees:** Many barndo dreamers don't always realize that permits aren't free. And, in some cases, you'll require more than one—sewer permit, electrical permit, building permit and the list goes on. Depending on where you live, these permits could tally up to thousands of dollars. As with everything else, make the price inquiries part of your initial research when assessing the area.

- **Utility Connections:** Your intention might be to connect your property to local sewer, water and gas lines. In some instances, this might require the relevant companies to come out and connect these utilities. In instances where your home will be too rural to connect to local supplies, you might have to have systems installed.

- **Cable & Internet Costs:** Whether you're going to install internet, cable, or both you'll have to get these installed.

- **Creating Access Roads:** If your property is far off from the usual roads, you might have to pay contractors to create an access road for your team to reach your property.

- **Temporary Rental Costs:** Delays with your construction process can come in the form of rainy weather, delays with supply deliveries and issues with contractors. This only really has an impact on your budget if you're renting a different place while you're waiting for your barndo to be completed.

- **Unforeseen Building Costs:** All the planning in the world can't prevent a few unforeseen building mishaps that may need repairing or replacing. Windows can accidentally break, a plumbing pipe can be too short, and some floor materials may need replacing—the list is endless.

Money Saving Tips

Diving into your barndo project is very exciting. After all, you're finally building your dream home. As you set up your budget and do your costing calculations for probably the hundredth time, it's important to note there are several significant ways that you can save some money in the process. We've compiled a list of tips that you should consider as you create your budget.

Build Your Barndo in a Cheaper State

Barndominium prices vary, depending on the state you opt for. That means it could be considerably easier to build your barndo in some states than others. With that said, we've included a list of the cheapest states to consider.

U.S. State	Estimated Cost Per Square Foot
West Virginia	$81
Alabama	$86
Ohio	$93
Texas	$95
Nebraska	$96
Louisiana	$97
Iowa	$97
Idaho	$99
North Dakota	$135
Mississippi	$150
Michigan	$150

Opt for a Barndo Kit

If you are on a less-than-friendly budget, you might have to shelve your pack of custom plans in favor of a barndominium kit. Essentially, a barndo kit is a prefabricated kit based on standard designs. A huge plus point with kits is that they come with just about everything you need. You can expect the following in a kit:

- Steel frame (often called a shell)
- Exterior sheets that form your barndo's walls
- Trim that attaches your sheets to your frame
- Closures such as doors and windows (these will always be standard size)
- Different interior layouts

Kits cost less than sourcing each product separately and there's also no need to aggravate yourself by dealing with multiple vendors and different shipping dates and times. Everything arrives in a wrapped pallet, ready for assembly.

Another plus point about kits is that they're available in a wide variety of designs, layouts and sizes. Choosing between a 2-bedroom plan is as easy as choosing a 5+ option. Different kit suppliers will have different options at varying prices. If you're opting for a kit, be sure to shop around for the best price. (We take a more in-depth look at barndo kits in a later chapter)

Clear the Property Yourself

Depending on how rural you're going with your barndo dream, it might be necessary to clear the land to make it accessible for your construction team. If your contracting team needs to clear the area before they start building, that work will be added to your bill.

To avoid the extra costs, it may be time to rustle up some of your younger relatives to help you clear the area. Dig out the necessary plants and remove as much rubble as you can. Keep the plants in a container of water and keep them for replanting around your barndo. You'll save on having to buy new plants when you start with the landscaping process.

Purchase Your Own Supplies and Building Materials

If you have limited experience with building or supplies and materials, you might be tempted to hand the reins over to your contractor. After all, he probably knows what's best. Right? Yes and no.

Allowing your contractor to be in charge of buying the building materials will limit the control you have over how much is spent. Your subcontractor is also less likely to phone or drive around for better prices. These guys generally have their own preferred suppliers and will always use them whenever possible. This might not always do your budget any favors.

Speak to your contractor in advance. Get a list of the required materials in the correct sizes and quantities. Be sure to buy these supplies well in advance to avoid having contractors with nothing to do while they wait for materials to arrive.

Opt for Standard Sized Doors and Windows

Barndos are incredibly popular because they are highly customizable. However, it's crucial to note that customization comes with a price tag. Simple features such as doors and windows can really push up your overall prices if you opt for bigger, wider versions. It's always a good idea to opt for standard sizes as a way to keep your budget under control.

Most barndos are constructed with steel columns spaced between 6 and 12 feet apart. The main purpose of these wider spaces is to enable you to add wider doors and windows. Remember that anything bigger than the standard size will push up the construction and installation prices. Instead of opting for large doors all around your barndo, opt for one statement entry door with standard options for the rest.

Another point to keep in mind with bigger windows is that you'll need bigger (or more) curtains, blinds or drapes. Therefore, opting for standard-sized windows will save you money in two areas.

Analyze DIY Options

You don't have to be a master DIY builder to do some of the work around your building project by yourself. Smaller tasks such as painting, drywalling or cleaning up may easily be within your reach. The more you can do yourself, the less likely you will be to have to pay someone to do it.

Experts agree that opting to do some of the building tasks as DIY work combined with major cost-effective decisions can show an impressive saving of $83,268. Review the list of work that needs to be done and determine which you'll be able to do yourself.

Shop Around for a Reputable Contractor

Never accept the first quote you receive when you start approaching builders and contractors. Always shop around for experienced and reputable contractors and subcontractors.

While it may seem expensive at the onset, it will save you a lot of money in the long run. Choosing a contractor with little experience may leave you having to hire another more experienced team to finalize the build.

Additionally, most contractors have a well-established network of reliable subcontractors such as plumbers, electricians and roofers. Additionally, a reputable contractor will be insured with the right certifications in place. In the event of a job site injury, this will limit your liability. Furthermore, a well-known contractor will most likely be able to help you with getting the necessary permits without too much runaround.

Repurpose Existing Furniture

Moving out of your existing little house in the city doesn't mean you need to discard all your existing furniture. While it's true that you will have a new, bigger space, you can easily repurpose what you already have.

Furniture and cabinets are items that you can buy down the line. For the most part, these items shouldn't be on your 'must-have' list, especially if the bulk of the budget has already been allocated to the building process.

If you have to buy kitchen cabinets, it's a great idea to opt for ready-to-assemble options from local wholesalers. Since kitting out your kitchen with new cabinets is often one of the more extensive costs, deciding the ready-to-assemble rather than a whole new build will save you an average between $2,500 and $24,000.

Consider Effective Ways to Recover Some Building Costs

One of the most effective ways to deal with a hectic building budget is to recover some of the initial costs. A simple way to do this is to consider adding a mother-in-law suite next to your barndo. Alternatively, you can also divide a section of your barndo into a few rentable rooms or living spaces. By renting these spaces you can easily recover some costs.

How Are Barndominiums Taxed?

Unfortunately, barndominiums are taxed in all states across the U.S. As with so many other factors on your barndo journey, the amount you'll pay will depend on where you live. In fact, it's not uncommon for two barndo owners in the same state to pay varying prices, simply because of where they live.

Essentially, the barndo tax process is one of the aspects that can get tricky. In most cases, tax appraisers will base your evaluation on the floor measurement. On the other hand, some states will evaluate everything on the land.

We've included several important tips that could make your tax process a whole lot simpler:

- **Request the Property's Tax Card:** Keep a copy of your tax card for any appeals or queries with the tax assessor. A copy should be readily available at the local assessor's office and includes all the data of your property. It will also show any details that were included in the last assessment. You can query the ones you don't agree with.

- **Consider Additions to the Structure:** If you're challenging the last tax assessment done on your property, it's a good idea to hold off on any additions that could push the bill up.

- **Check Your Neighbors:** If there are other barndos in the area, you can request evaluation statistics to compare your assessment.

Pro Tip: *When you're shortlisting your favorite location options, be sure to check the tax regulations for that particular state. Knowing what you're up against will save you a whole lot of stressful situations down the line.*

Other Important Costs to Keep in Mind

Aside from taxes on your actual barndo, there are a few other costs you shouldn't forget about. These include the following:

- **Property Taxes:** The value of property taxes again depends on the area you live in. Be sure to request the average cost of this when you're doing the other research for your specific area.

- **Loan Interest:** The type of loan you take out to finance your barndo could leave with a loan interest to pay monthly. It's important to factor these costs into your monthly calculations.

- **Insurance:** If you're building your barndo and financing it through a lender, it's important to have property insurance. These types of insurance cover natural disasters, fire damage and theft among others.

- **Monthly Utilities:** Depending on the setup of your barndo, you might have to pay monthly utilities for water and energy. To avoid these costs, it might be a good idea to look into solar energy and energy-efficient appliances. (We'll discuss these in later chapters)

Key Takeaway

When you're creating your budget, a few important key takeaways include:

- Choose one of the cheaper states to build your barndo.
- Opt for a barndo kit rather than a custom build.
- Purchase materials and supplies to save costs and opt for standard sizes where possible.
- Get estimates on all permits, additions and labor costs before beginning the process.
- Include monthly costs such as utilities, loan interest and insurance in your calculations.
- Review DIY options on your barndo build as this will save considerable costs.
- Establish a list of jobs that are necessary versus tasks you can do as you go along.

- Speak to a professional about the tax expectations in your area.

Once you've established a budget, it's time to move on to your lending and financing options. Our next chapter will cover these options in extensive detail.

Chapter 3: Financing

Wanting a barndominium is one thing. But unless you already have the money saved up, getting the financing to pay for your dream home is another kettle of fish altogether. For many first-time barndo owners, finding the right lender and securing the funds can be very frustrating, sometimes even impossible to secure.

There is, however, some good news. While it's not always easy to secure financing for your barndo, it's not impossible. In fact, there are a variety of different options to consider. We've dedicated a whole chapter to assisting you with finding the right lender.

Furthermore, we've included some expert tips to improve your credit score. To assist you in choosing the right financing option, we'll also be reviewing the difference between a 15-year loan vs. a 30-year loan. Let's dive right in.

Why Are Regular Lenders Reluctant to Finance Barndos

When we set out on our journey to find the best lender to help us fulfill our barndo dream, we were quite surprised by how difficult it was in some instances. In fact, it was one of the top hiccups we had to work around. At times it felt as though we weren't quite getting our dream across and that perhaps it wasn't meant to be. One thing we learnt from the financing part of our journey was perseverance!

If you've ever applied for a regular home loan, you have some idea of what to expect. Depending on your credit score, getting a regular home loan is often easier than most people think. But you're not building a regular home, are you? If you've already started researching lender options, you'd have found out that traditional lenders such as banks are often oddly reluctant to finance barndominiums. Why is this?

Barndo dreamers often encounter unexpected obstacles when they set out to find the perfect lender for the job. This is mostly because many conventional lenders don't have experience with construction loans required to build steel structures. Your best bet is often to broaden your search to rural credit unions or farm banks.

Are You Having a Hard Time Finding a Lender?

It's important to note that finding a lender can often be very challenging. Sometimes, it can be downright discouraging. For the most part, this can simply be attributed to not knowing which avenues to follow.

Struggling to find a lender to finance your barndo shouldn't leave you feeling like you want to give up on your dream. At some point, all barndominium owners were where you are right now. **The secret is to not**

quit. With the right preparation, you'll eventually find a lender prepared to assist with a construction loan. We've listed a few options worth trying.

Banks or Credit Unions

For many people, a bank or credit union is the first port of call because these places have most likely financed all your other credit. Despite being a loyal customer of these institutions, the reality is that you might not have much success here.

This is generally because many traditional lenders don't regard barndos as a sound investment. However, that shouldn't stop you from starting with them. Barndo owners who have had favorable outcomes at these traditional facilities attribute their success to being well-prepared with the plans and bids they presented.

(We will discuss lender preparation later in this chapter)

Farm Credit

Chances are you're going to opt for a country setting to build your barndo. With that in mind, it's often easier to apply for a loan from a financial institution aimed at assisting American farmers.

Pro Tip: *Don't let your barndo loan application be the first type of business you do with this institution. Plan your finances in advance and be sure to consider this facility for some of your banking business. This way,* *they will know your credit rating and creditworthiness. It's often easier to ask for a loan from a lender that knows you and with whom you have an established record.*

Mortgage Brokers

Mortgage brokers are individuals that specialize in selling loan products from a variety of different lending facilities. Finding a broker that specializes in barndo mortgages will eliminate a big chunk of the legwork. However, be advised that they will most likely work on a commission basis. This will be an additional cost to add to your initial budget.

Mortgage Banks

Mortgage banks specialize in creating and servicing mortgage loans. This often includes barndominium loans. In the instance where the loan closes, the bank will sell the mortgage to a secondary mortgage holder. One of the top perks of this type of bank is that they offer greater lending facilities and provide access to better interest rates.

Online Loan Entities

With the explosion of e-commerce all over the internet, it was only a matter of time before getting a loan became as easy as logging in online. These online options offer a wide variety of financial products to anyone who qualifies. Since they're affiliated with reputable national or international banks, they can offer mortgage loans. The only drawback here might be the value of the loan. It might not be as much as you need, but there's no harm in checking with a few of the more popular options.

Facebook Recommendations

Another simple way to get potential recommendations is to join Facebook barndo groups. Speak to barndominium builders and owners who have already passed the financing stage. They will advise you on a host of new options as well as all the requirements to move through the lending phase with as little stress as possible.

New Century Bank

A popular recommendation from a popular Facebook group points potential barndo owners toward a national lending company called New Century Bank. While we have no personal dealings with these guys, it's worth noting that they have a 5-star rating from the prestigious Bankrate.com.

They also have an app that could make the whole process so much easier. If you're working through a list of options, this one might be worth looking into.

Rural 1st

Another popular Facebook recommendation that we stumbled across is for a lending company called Rural 1st.

What makes this option appealing is that they boast "financing post-frame and non-conforming homes the same way as conventional style-homes."

They also offer both fixed-rate and variable construction loans. Their Facebook page also boasts helpful articles for people starting out on their barndo journey.

Colt Building & Homes

As a barndo design company that offers in house financing in all 50 states, Colt Buildings & Homes is a firm favorite on several Facebook groups. They offer VA, USDA, Bridge and FHA loans. The fact that they also offer barndo designs and kits makes it an ideal option for people who don't want to deal with too many different vendors.

Ask Your Builder for Recommendations

Part of your initial planning involves consulting with builders who have experience in the barndo building industry. This is crucial as you'll need to determine the labor and potential product costs.

During this consultation, make a point of asking the builder for recommendations of lenders that previous customers have had success with. You can also ask them for the contact details of a few of their previous customers. Speaking to the barndo owners in the area may turn out to be a momentous help as they can provide tips for dealing with all the various steps involved in building your dream barndo.

Meeting With a Lender—Preparation Is Key

Preparation is key when you're making appointments with various lenders. You want to give yourself the best possible chance of getting the right loan. Be sure to prepare and collect the following documents.

- **Approved Floor Plans:** Floor plans which include blueprints and schematics.
- **Accredited Appraisals:** Property appraisal which shows the value of the property as it stands as well as how much it will be worth once the project is complete.
- **Utility List:** Utilities that are existing on the property as well as the new ones that will be added.
- **Contractor Estimates:** Bids and estimates from the contractor—it may be a good idea to get estimates from three contractors to show the lender you have done your homework.
- **Structure Product List:** An extensive list of products and resources you'll need to complete the job—a professional list on a store or supplier letterhead will be more professional than simply scrawling the list on a piece of paper.

- **Timeline Report:** Include a report showing estimated timelines of how long each phase will take to complete.
- **Permit Requests:** Documents from the county or state showing that permits have been requested or received for the property.
- **Credit Score Documents:** Any documents or statements that add to the strength of your credit score.
- **Proof of Down Payment:** Bank statements reflecting the required down payment—proving to the lender that you have the down payment might increase your chances of success.

We recommend making your package of documents be neat and concise. Provide details and contact details for all vendors and suppliers. This will make it easy for the lender to do verifications if they need to.

You need to create a level of confidence with the lender that your potential project is well-planned with realistic goals. Most times, the more preparation you do, the easier the process will be.

Useful Tips on Improving Credit Score to Secure Better Financing Rates

One of the top deciding factors that will determine how easy it is to secure a loan is your credit score. If your credit score is not quite where you'd like it to be, there are several steps you can take to improve your current rating.

According to a recent article from myknowledgebroker.com and nerwallet.com, you should easily be able to improve your existing credit score by at least 100 points. All you have to do is follow a few simple guidelines, which we'll discuss in some detail below.

Assess Your Credit Record: *Request an updated copy of your most recent credit record from the three US credit reporting agencies. Simply email annualcreditreport.com to request information from TransUnion, Equifax and Experian. Check for errors and reasons for a lower credit score. This will identify the problems you need to work on.*

Catch Up on Past-Due Bills: *Once you have assessed your accounts, make a list of all the past-due bills. These are the accounts that you will start updating to get current as soon as possible. Doing this is the fastest way to improve your credit score. However, ignoring or delaying this step will set you back or minimize the number of lender options available to you.*

Pay Current Bills Timeously: *While you're catching up on your past-due bills, it's crucial to avoid letting other accounts fall by the wayside. An easy way to stay in control of this is to opt for your bank's bill pay service. Request electronic statements to be emailed to you so that you can keep track of your payments.*

Get a Handle on Your Credit Cards: *When you're planning your dream barndo, it's very hard not to go out on a shopping spree to buy many decorations and accessories! However, until you have a lender secured, it's best to take it easy with credit card purchases. Essentially, you want to keep your credit card balances below 10 percent for each line of credit. Keeping your balances low will secure a couple of additional points.*

Clear as Much of Your Current Debt: *One of the best ways to improve your credit score is to minimize the amount of debt you have. Start with the smallest balances you have and work toward settling them as soon as possible. When you've settled an account, use the installment of that account to pay past-due bills or to pay off the next small balance on your list.*

Have a Variety of Credit Types: *For the most part, your credit score in the US is calculated using what's known as the FICO score. According to experts, the FICO calculator awards higher scores to consumers with a mixture of credit cards and installment loans. This proves that you can maintain different interest rates. That said, it's a good idea to have at least one running credit card and one or two installment loans. Be careful to not overdo it as this will have a negative effect on your score.*

Don't Request Too Many Credit Reports: *Pick a few consecutive days to perform all your credit inquiries. This will avoid the FICO scoring system from* *mistaking your inquiries as your attempt to open multiple lines of credit.*

Refrain From Adding New Credit Applications: *Remember that the goal is to improve your credit score in order to find a lender to finance the whole amount required for your barndo. Try by all means to not open any additional accounts until you have secured the barndo financing.*

Keep Paid-Up Accounts Open: *As you work through your credit list, it might be tempting to close accounts that you have paid off. However, keeping them open and unused shows potential lenders that you can manage your credit wisely. Similarly, keeping older credit cards open provides you with a longer credit history, which is also beneficial to your score.*

Invest in a Secured Credit Card: *Another effective way to improve your credit is by using a secured credit card. In short, this type of credit card allows you to pay an amount of money upfront. The deposit amount determines the credit limit. It's important to note that seeing the effects of this type of card could take several months. So, while this might not be in your short-term plan, to secure funds for your barndo, having this card and depositing money into it will create a savings system that you can fall back on down the line.*

How Do Amortization Schedules Work with Home Loans

When you're discussing and planning to finance your barndo dream, it's equally important to consider how current amortization schedules work with home loans. If that sounds like a mouthful, it might help if we backtrack a few steps.

What Is an Amortization Schedule?

In short, an amortization schedule is a table that depicts every periodic loan payment that is owed. An amortized loan displays a level of payment over the loan's lifespan. These assist individuals with better budgeting their cash flow over the period of the loan.

Another advantage of amortized loans is that the principal component is always included in each payment. That allows the outstanding balance to be reduced over time.

How Does a 30-Year Amortization Schedule Work?

For the first stages of a 30-year loan, the repayments go toward the principal or interest of the 360-month period. For the latter part of the loan, the repayment will go toward covering the original principal debt. Your lender will provide this schedule as a table or chart. Essentially, the amortization can be viewed as being the depreciation of your barndo loan.

30-Year Loan vs. 15-Year Loan

One of the common questions barndo dreamers often ask us has to do with the difference between 15 and 30-year loans. Well, here it is.

Traditional Mortgage Loan

Conventional loans make up about 90% of regular home mortgages in the US. These loans are done over a 30-year period and feature a lower repayment installment but a higher interest rate. However, lenders rarely want to provide barndo loans under this option. This is mostly because many lenders don't regard barndos as traditional homes. They will probably offer you a construction loan.

Construction Loan

A construction loan from a bank, credit union and farm credit institution has a higher repayment installment and is only available for shorter terms.

That means that if you choose this option, you'll be looking at a maximum period of 15 years. The shorter repayment term means you'll pay less interest at a much lower rate.

Besides your 15-year period, your barndo financing will be divided into two phases.

Phase 1: The construction loan is mostly a one-year loan that must be used for the primary construction costs.

Phase 2: This part refers to the permanent loan which should finance the remaining building costs. Your new monthly payment will now be based on the outstanding amount on the construction loan. The original loan for the property will be included here as well.

Essentially, this means that the construction loan turns into a permanent mortgage once the structure is completed. From then on, you'll decide on an adjustable or fixed interest rate, but with fixed payments. At this point, your construction invariably turns into a regular mortgage loan. A key difference is that the lender (or bank) will provide checks at predetermined intervals to pay for all the construction costs as they arise.

Many barndo owners recommend opting for the 30-year loan because the repayment installment is much lower. In the event of an unforeseen financial burden, you'll e be glad you opted for the lower installment. If you have the money, you can always double or even triple your installment to pay in advance.

Down Payment Options

Most lenders will require a down payment varying between 20–40 percent of the required loan. If you haven't already started saving for this, it should be bumped up to your top priority. Don't be discouraged if you think this is going to take some time.

While you're working on generating and saving your down payment, you can work on the rest of the planning aspects. There's always the option of borrowing your down payment. However, we don't recommend doing this as it will just increase the amount you need to pay back. The best option here would be to save until you have the required amount.

How Do Interest Rates Affect the Loan?

There isn't a set interest rate for your barndominium loan. Factors such as your credit score, credit history and the requested loan amount will determine the interest rate. Various lenders may also have different interest rates available. Homeowners can also choose whether they'd prefer a fixed or adjustable interest rate.

Opting for an adjustable-rate mortgage (ARM) has fluctuating rate changes. They might seem appealing because they often have lower monthly payments than a fixed-rate mortgage. However, your monthly payments could sometimes go up by quite a lot. This can be hectic if you're working on a specific monthly budget.

Securing your finance is possibly the most difficult stage of getting your barndominium dream started. Once the finance is secured, the fun part really starts!

Key Takeaways

- Assess your credit record before you approach lenders.
- Rectify any bad credit or overdue accounts to increase your credit score.
- Thorough preparation is key—obtain all relevant documents to create a strong project plan.
- Research various lending options including farm credit lenders and online options.

Review various repayment options and consider the long-term effects of each.

Chapter 4: Your Dream Location

Whether you're a barndo dreamer or not, everyone has an ideal place they would love to live if circumstances allowed. It could be a farm setting with picturesque views of lush mountain views and lakes flowing nearby. Or it could be a rural setting close enough to the city to still enjoy all the amenities but far away enough to have your own, large, wonderful and private space.

For us, deciding to set our dream Barndo up in Texas was a no-brainer. Aside from its picturesque views and wide-open fields, the easy zoning laws made Texas an ideal site to build the Cohen Barndo! As a bonus, we get to enjoy all the outdoor activities that the Cohen clan just loves to get into. Weekends filled with swimming, boating and cliff jumping make us wish we'd moved to the country sooner. Living in the country, with our fun activities literally down the road, life really is one long vacation for us these days!

Many barndominium builders embrace the barndo concept because it's a great way to run a small to medium business close to your home. That said, the type of business you'll be running might determine the location you should be looking into.

For instance, if you want to start a winery, you might want to consider a location close to the wine-rich Napa Valley. Alternatively, if you want to fulfill your dream of owning a riding school, Texas could be a perfect choice. Since zoning laws and state regulations might restrict certain locations, it helps to know where the current hot spots are for barndo dreamers. Let's take a look at some of the current, more popular locations.

Types of Locations to Consider

A recent article published by Barndominium Life highlights a few of the top locations Barndo dreamers are considering. While we believe Texas is the perfect place to build your barndo dream, we've decided to share several of these locations with you to broaden your options.

Houston, Texas

For folks who still want to be in close proximity to vibrant city life, Houston is a wonderful option. The features that make Houston a top barndo location contender are highlighted below.

1. Ample available land.

2. Perfect balance between city and country living.

3. No zoning laws regarding land use.

4. Limited restrictions on building development.

5. Climate consists of long hot summers with cold and windy winters.

6. The area is not really prone to snow.

7. Close proximity to the American space program.

NW Arkansas

If it's mountains you're looking for, rumor has it that you can't get any better than the Ozark Mountains in NW Arkansas. Take a look at the top reasons to consider building a barndo in this picturesque part of the world.

1. One of the top areas to embrace the barndominium concept.

2. Rich cultural heritage.

3. Popular attractions include the Museum of American Art, Crystal Bridges and the Hobbs State Park-Conservation Area.

4. Climate includes hot summers and cold winters with snow.

5. Zoning laws in place that could restrict the size, number of stories, location and height of barndos.

Fort Worth & Weatherford, Texas

Another two Texan towns stand out as top barndo choices for a few obvious reasons. Read on to see why Fort Worth and Weatherford are equally wonderful options to consider.

1. Close proximity to the hustle and bustle of Dallas, making it close enough for children who need to attend school.

2. Both cities feature a considerably lower crime rate than most other Texas cities, making it an ideal place for your family as well to run a business.

3. Wide open spaces make it easy to find the perfect spot of land for your barndo

4. Affordable to build and customize barndos in Texas.

5. Liberal zoning laws make customization easy and even accommodate barndo business ventures.

6. Several skilled barndo contractors in the area with extensive experience could be valuable to your barndominium project.

Tuscaloosa, Alabama

There seem to be two major attractions to building a barndo in Alabama. The first is the beautiful landscape. The second, and probably most important reason is the affordable pricing. The average barndominium cost in Alabama can range anywhere from $30 to $40 per square foot.

If you've started looking at barndo cost models, then you'll know this price range is top-notch. Moreover, the lower your initial cost, the easier it is to expand and create an incredible amount of customizations. This is excellent news for barndo builders who want a truly unique dream home. What else makes Alabama an excellent location to consider?

1. Temperate climate with hot and sunny summers and moderate winters.

2. Cost-effective barndo prices.

3. Many reputable barndominium builders in the area make it easy to find the right contractor.

4. Near to the Museum of Natural History and Moundville Archeological Park (if that sort of thing interests you, of course).

5. Ideal for barndo dreamers looking for breathtaking views.

Edmond, Oklahoma

If the growing barndo community sprouting up all over Texas isn't for you, then perhaps you'd like to explore the vast open plains of Oklahoma. Like Texas, Oklahoma has a lot to offer. Having grown up in Oklahoma, I can vouch for the picturesque views, low cost of living and tons of outdoor activities on offer. Here are more reasons why Oklahoma is one of the top barndo location options.

1. Close proximity to popular attractions such as Armstrong Auditorium and Arcadia Lake.
2. Regarded by many as one of the top locations to build a barndo.
3. An atmosphere of relaxed living, making it the ideal place to escape the rat race.
4. Breathtaking landscape views.
5. Inexpensive to build barndos with prices ranging from $60 to $90 per square foot.
6. Several specialized builders in the area.
7. Edmond is regarded as among the top school districts.

A rural area is situated close enough to the town to be near all the local amenities that you and your family might need.

Waco, Texas

Well known for its natural landscape and exquisite attractions, Waco is fast becoming a top location for making barndominium dreams come true. Here's why it's worth adding to your shortlist.

1. Attractions include Waco Mammoth National Monument and the oldest suspension bridge in Texas.

2. Picturesque landscape as far as the eye can see.

3. Prices to build barndos start at $100 per square foot.

4. Many skilled barndo builders in the area.

5. Lax zoning laws make it the best place to build highly customized barndos.

6. Ideal location for a traditional, country style barndo.

Springfield, Missouri

Another place to consider outside of Texas is without a doubt Missouri. It's an ideal spot for the barndo builder who wants to get as far away from city life as possible.

1. Ideal location for nature and wildlife enthusiasts.

2. Close proximity to the Wonders of Wildlife National Museum and Dickerson Park Zoo.

3. A network of underground caves makes it a wonderful hiking and picnic area

4. Initial costs of a barndo vary from $30-$40 per square foot making it ideal for barndo builders working on a tighter budget.

5. The climate in Missouri includes hot summers as well as cold, snowy winters.

6. The area doesn't have many mountain ranges so it's not particularly suited to people looking for high mountain backdrops.

It's evident from the many locations situated in Texas, that we're not the only people who regard this state to be the ideal place to create your barndominium dream. If you love the outdoors as much as we do it might be worth considering the move.

Wide open spaces and gorgeous landscapes enhance our love of cliff jumping and swimming. The expert builders and reasonable zoning laws were just a huge bonus. If you're still on the fence about choosing a location, Texas should be close to the top of your list.

Types of Weather to Consider

Many people claim that weather isn't really a factor when choosing the perfect location. However, it's been our experience that the wrong type of weather year-round can put a damper on your barndominium dream. How does the climate in a potential location determine its popularity?

Sunny: *Most barndo dreamers we've met seem to prefer a predominantly sunny climate. That's because a barndo in the country comes with so many outdoor possibilities. Hiking, horse riding, picnics, swimming, fishing—the list seems endless! Furthermore, if you're going to be* *running a business such as a winery or farmers market, you're going to need as much sun as possible.*

Snow: *Most people enjoy a bit of snow. It's great for cooling things down. But for most people, there's a limit to the snow they can handle. If you're one of those people, a barndo in Alaska might not be what you're looking for. If you're going to opt for a location with high snowfall, you might have to look into having your barndo structure specially treated to prevent damage from excessive snow. This is usually the case when you opt for pole structures. Living in a high snowfall area might also require additional insulation and even underfloor heating. Both of these aspects will influence your initial budget.*

Desert: *Fancy a barndo in Nevada? As tempting as that may sound, it's not everyone's cup of tea. Be sure to consider the pros and cons of living in or close to a desert location. You also need to assess how this will affect any business you want to run on your property. Desert climate comes with warmer temperatures. How will this affect your animals or crops?*

Rainy: *Locations that have a predominantly rainy climate also have their drawbacks. They may also not be an ideal climate to raise children and animals in. After all, who wants to stay indoors all day? If you're considering a location in a high rainfall area, it'll be a good idea to consider an enclosed porch around your* *barndo. That way you'll be able to enjoy some of the outdoors, even on the rainiest of days.*

How Important Is Zoning

The purpose of zoning in certain areas is to regulate land and property markets to create a balanced community environment. Essentially, setting up zoning laws prevents land waste by dividing areas for specific uses. Zoning laws also limit factors such as building heights and also prevent manufacturing plants from setting up shops in residential neighborhoods.

The important factor to remember about zoning laws is that they don't apply everywhere. In other instances, zoning laws vary in different states. We recommend checking local and state laws requiring zoning in the area you want to build your barndo. After you've identified a potential area, check the zoning laws before you start drawing up plans.

If you're going to be using a general contractor to manage the building process, the good news is that they can pull the necessary zoning permits. For the most part that will take some of the stress off your shoulders!

What Factors Are Essential for Your Barndo Location?

Choosing your barndo location depends on what you need around you to have a comfortable life. For many people, building away from the city is the preferred choice. This is because there's more space, easier access to outdoor activities and it's removed from the rush of city life.

Barndo dreamers with children of school-going age will need to be close to the local schools. To help you choose the must-have factors of your location, we've listed a few common deal breakers that were important to us and our other barndo-building friends. It's important to draw up your own "Must have" list. Once you have this list, it's easy to start checking which locations meet all or most of your required criteria.

Proximity to Neighbors: *For some barndo dreamers, part of the attraction to a barndominium lifestyle is the vast amount of space between them and everyone else. Living in a barndo a considerable distance from neighbors ensures you all the privacy and solitude you could want. If you are going to run a business from your barndo, it's definitely a good idea to consider how close you want the neighbors to be.*

Nearby Amenities: *If you're currently living in a city or even a small town, there's no denying that you would have gotten used to certain amenities. Some of these would include parks to walk the dogs, fitness facilities and even coffee shops. How ready are you to give up your spot in the morning line at your local Starbucks? Would it bother you if you were no longer near the gym? On the plus side, with the space on offer in your new* *barndo, you can always create your own gym. The advantage of that is—the whole family gets to enjoy it!*

City Life: *Many people love the hustle and bustle of city life. The reality of the barndo concept is that the zoning laws of some states don't allow for barndominiums to be built in the city. Truth be told, if you're going to build a barndo small enough to fit on a city block, you may as well stick with a regular house. Alternatively, if you need to be near a city, you can pick a location that's within reasonable driving distance.*

Hiking: *Building a barndo in the great outdoors will provide you with access to hiking, bike trails and picnic spots. If this is something you and your family could get into, then country life might just be what you're looking for. As we've already mentioned, we enjoy the outdoors, and the ample hiking trails in Texas provide us with hours of entertainment.*

Beach: *When it comes to building a barndo, the only real limitations you face will be the zoning laws. But if you can find a beach in the area you're considering, what a bonus!*

Lakes: *Would you like your barndo to overlook a beautiful lake? Or be within walking distance? In addition to creating a picturesque view, having a lake nearby will be a wonderful way to connect with nature. For us, the nearby lakes allow us to indulge in our other family pastime—boating. Our dogs absolutely love visits* *to the lake, and we often joke that the dogs must wonder why we didn't move closer to the lake sooner.*

Mountains: *When we think of barndos in the mountains, we think of snowy peaks and lavish landscapes. Few things compare to the view of opening your barndo door and looking over a lavish mountain range. Aside from having a beautiful backdrop for your family photos, having lavish mountains are also excellent for those wonderful outdoor activities.*

Schools: *Do you have children of school-going age? Unless you're going to homeschool, you'll have to consider a location reasonably close to the local schools. Many locations are in close proximity to local towns, so finding a location that won't require sending the kids away to boarding school is easier than you think.*

Hospitals: *When you're drawing up your list of requirements for your perfect area, you might want to add access to hospitals and veterinary clinics if you're going to be raising animals on your property.*

How Easy Will It Be to Build in Your Preferred Location?

The ease at which your dream barndominium can be built primarily comes down to what exactly you want to do with the property and the structure. It should go without saying that a highly customized barndo with all the bells and whistles could run into some building snags. To some degree, these issues can be expected. However, there are others in your preferred location that you need to give due consideration to.

Will You Need to Have the Land and Soil Inspected?

Many barndominium builders often neglect to have the soil on their new property inspected. An unstable and uneven terrain can result in a sinking foundation down the line. Since foundations can be extremely expensive to repair once the structure has been built, it's crucial to check this before purchasing the property.

Essentially, the quality of the soil in the spot you're considering should easily be able to hold the weight and capacity of your home. The only way to determine this is to do a physical and composition test. Speak to your general contractor about the necessity for this in your area.

Many different factors can determine the quality of the soil you want to build your dream barndo on. A few of these include:

- Climate change in the area.
- The current quality of the soil (this includes assessing any factors that may be degrading the quality)

- Weather in the area and its effect on soil erosion—this is especially the case in rainy areas where increased soil erosion can be a cause for concern.
- How has the soil changed in the last 10 or even 20 years? This is crucial to know if your business involves planting crops of any kind.

Once the correct soil tests have been done, your building contractor will be able to assess the type of materials that can be used on the soil without causing any additional damage. For instance, an area with extensive soil moisture might lead to corrosion. In this case, you'd want to opt for corrosion-resistant materials.

How Accessible Are Public Utilities?

Access to public utilities such as running water and electricity will largely depend on where your chosen location is. If you're opting for a space deep into rural America, it's important to note that these luxuries aren't always a given.

As you choose your favorite spot, be sure to keep the following factors in mind:

- **Running Water:** *If running water isn't available at your location, you will need to drill a well. It's crucial to check the availability and cost of this before making it an option. Unfortunately, this isn't something that you can do after the barndo has been built. The reason for this is that* *barndominium plumbing is different from regular plumbing. Unlike regular plumbing pipes, barndo plumbing needs to be built into the foundation. Furthermore, adequate running water is a prerequisite to passing your final inspection. Without running water, you won't be able to move in.*

- **Sewer System**: *If your property isn't too far off the beaten path, you might still be able to link up to the nearest city sewer system. If you're going completely rural, you may have to build your own sewer system. As with the water, be sure to check costing before just agreeing to this as an option. The sewer plumbing pipes and fixtures will also have to be built into the foundation, so as with the water, this needs to be done first. If you're going to build your own system, this will use a sizable chunk of your initial budget.*

- **Electricity:** *Here you need to decide if you want to opt for a full solar system, taking you off the grid. Again, if you're not too far out of town, you'd still tap into the grid. While going off the grid is something you can do over time, you will need to have functioning electricity to pass your final inspection as well as run all your appliances. And, if you love baking as much as we do, having your kitchen appliance working is an absolute must-have!*

- **Cell Coverage:** *It's almost impossible to live without the internet these days. Especially if you're going to homeschool and communicate with family via Skype or Zoom. Moreover, if you're running a business out of your barndo, you'll need access to the internet. How far will your property be from the nearest cell coverage area? You might want to look into satellite internet. It's also a good idea to check with barndo homeowners in the area about the best and most affordable options they use.*

Are You Building a Business as Well?

If your barndo isn't just a dream home but a business as well, the type of business might dictate particular soil types. In most instances, wineries require special conditions to grow to have effective fruit. These are all factors that need to be considered.

Another factor worth considering is how accessible your barndo business is from the road. If your business will have customers or delivery drivers routinely coming in and out, you'll have to have a proper road between your barndo and the main road. Before settling on a barndo location, check road accessibility and how insulation affects your budget.

Pro tip: *Decide EXACTLY what you're going to do with your barndo. Establish if it's just a home or a business too. Create a list of the top conditions you need for your* *home and your business. (List the minimum conditions you'll settle for as well) Compare that to the types of businesses in the area. If there aren't any wineries or nurseries in the area, it might be because the soil or climate isn't compatible. Check how the climate will affect any potential animals. Speak to existing barndo residents and contractors before you settle on a location.*

Key Takeaways

When it comes to choosing your dream location, here are the key takeaways to consider:

- Determine what purpose your barndominium will serve—home, business or a combination of both.
- Decide what amenities you'll need and which you can live not so close to.
- Check the weather of your potential area and decide if it suits your lifestyle, business and recreational activities.
- Before you set your heart on a picturesque location, check the zoning laws in that area—remember that some areas are more flexible than others.
- Some areas will require soil inspections to ensure there are no structural issues with your barndominium down the road.

- Speak to other barndo owners in the area to establish what, if any, snags they encountered during their barndo building journey—be sure to ask them about the pros and cons of the area, the weather and the amenities in general—you can compile a list of the things barndo residents wish they'd known about the location before moving there. Join Facebook groups of barndo owners in the areas on your shortlist.

One thing we learned during our barndo journey is that you can't make too many lists or do too many comparisons and ask too many questions. After all, the last thing you want is to be halfway through the building process only to discover that the negatives outweigh the positives. When it comes to choosing the perfect location, research is definitely your friend.

Chapter 5: Hiring the Right Team

Have you given any serious thought to who you'll hire to put your barndo dream together? Once you've secured your financing and decided on the perfect location, it's time to choose the people who will be helping you not only create your dream but also help you save money in the process.

We were very lucky in this instance. I grew up in Oklahoma as part of a working family. That meant, helping my dad with household projects soon became second nature. My dad would always be busy with home improvement projects, and I don't mean just painting a wall here and digging up a flower bed there. He would often decide to break out a wall dividing say the kitchen and dining area, in order to create an open plan and more social family environment. I would see him planning, measuring, and calling peers for advice. He would talk about how he could knock out a certain wall without hassle, but that other wall along that main entrance would need reinforcement.

We delighted in wearing miniature safety gear at times—and getting big hammers and told to just go wild and bash that wall to the ground. That was a lot of fun until we were tasked with assisting in loading the rubble into wheelbarrows to dump into the landfill at the other end of our property. A seemingly tedious task, until I realized later on in life this is a great way to reinforce a foundation or fill an unwanted pool or for other forms of creative landscaping.

When I started working, it was almost a given that I'd follow the general contractor route. It was not only something I had a great deal of experience in, but it became a passion of mine. There was nothing quite like the absolute thrill of drawing up plans which were tailored to the exact needs and circumstances of the client. And then the even greater thrill of these plans panning out and the work literally going according to plan.

Sure, this was not always the case, but those instances where things went wrong were where I gained the most experience and learned the most about my abilities, and this is where my skills and abilities grew. The best stories do not come from the projects that were smooth sailing, but from the ones where things went wrong. That said, years of not only finding but working with great teams gave me the experience needed to jump in and make our dream a reality, without getting stuck with shoddy contractors.

Not everyone has been so lucky though. Between us, we've heard some scary stories about barndo owners having their dreams dashed by inexperienced contractors just out to make a quick buck. With that in mind, we've decided to share some valuable tips about finding the right team.

You'll find this section especially useful if your barndo is your first-ever building project. Even if you've had some experience with contractors and DIY, it's always helpful to get a few tips that may end up saving you money in the long run.

What Type of Contractors Will You Need and What Do They Do?

When it comes to hiring the right team, the first point of business is knowing what needs to be done and who needs to do it. Don't forget that for your new home to pass the occupancy certification, certain jobs, such as plumbing and electrical need to be done by professionals.

Furthermore, we should also highlight that in 2022, the average labor cost for barndominium construction varied between $100 and $200 per square foot. That means that a small barndo of 1,200 square foot will cost anywhere from $12,000 to $24,000 in labor costs alone. With that in mind, it's crucial to have the right people on hand to do the job properly the first time around.

To simplify the process, we're going to give you a rundown of the key players in your barndo building journey.

General Contractor

In short, a general contractor is a person responsible for overseeing the entire project. They will generally arrange the subcontractors and will supervise the work that needs to be done. Here you have two options. You can hire a general contractor (with all the experience needed, but at a cost) or you can be your own general contractor. (More on this later)

On average, hiring a general contractor for your barndo build can cost anywhere between $150 to $190 per square foot, as opposed to about $95 per square foot for a DIY job.

Architect/Draftsperson

An architect or draftsperson is the person who draws up the plans for your barndominium. Even when you're opting for a pre-designed kit, you may need an architect.

This is because some states require that barndo owners only use plans that have been completed by professionals who know about the area's zoning rules. For the most part, this is because barndos are considered non-conventional buildings. It's also a requirement in the building of two-story barndos.

Plumber

A plumber is a person responsible for ensuring that your barndo has running water, and flushing toilets. They also need to install any plumbing pipes and fixtures. If your property is close enough to the county mains, the plumbing team will simply hook you up to it.

If your building is situated too far from the mains, the team will have to build a plumbing set-up from scratch. Plumbing labor and materials will depend on the type of job that needs to be done, and the number of fixtures that need to be installed. Generally, the average amount for plumbing ranges from $4000 upwards.

Electrician

If you want your barndo to have lights and working appliances, you will need a certified electrical team. These are the guys that install the necessary wiring and cables throughout your barndo to ensure that you have power at the flick of a switch. They also need to ensure that all electrical work is done according to state regulations.

As with plumbing, the electrical work has no fixed amount. It also depends on the type of work, amount of cabling, wiring and outlets that need to be installed. If you have appliances and a water heater that need to be connected, that will be extra. Unfortunately, unless you are certified, the electrical and plumbing aspects shouldn't be done as DIY jobs.

Drywaller

Since most barndos are designed with an open-plan layout, there aren't many walls that need to be put up. In the instances where you might need a wall, it will most likely be drywall, typically made of gypsum. You will need a drywaller to hang the walls where you want them.

Painter

It's highly unlikely that you're going to leave your barndo with only the bare steel frame it comes in. That means the painting will also need to be done. Here you also have two options. Either do the painting yourself (and save on the labor costs) or hire a professional painter to do the job for you.

Should You Act as Your Own General Contractor?

When you're looking at the top ways to stay within budget on your barndo project, the number piece of advice that most people will give you is to be your own general contractor. While this may be true, it isn't always the best idea. We will tell you why.

As a general contractor, you'll spend an average of 25 to 40 hours a week organizing, monitoring and reviewing the building project. That means you'll be overseeing everyone from electricians to the guy installing the windows. Additionally, you'll be ordering your own supplies, following up on deliveries and above all else keeping the project within budget.

It sounds easy enough. If you have done it before and assuming you're available during the building process, it might be worth venturing into. However, for people who still have to go to a regular 9 to 5 job between the barndo building, it may not be such a good idea. Let's run through some of the pros and cons to consider.

Pros

- Could save you money as you're not paying a general contractor.
- Being in control of buying supplies gives you control over your budget.
- You can do some of the easier tasks yourself, saving money on subcontractors (painting, laying floors and landscaping are good examples of this).
- There's the satisfaction of doing it yourself.
- You're in control of the planning and execution process.
- Depending on your schedule, you can arrange subcontractors to work at times that suit your plan—there's no rush and no chaos of having a bunch of different contractors in each other's way.

Cons

- In some states, lenders and banks forbid owners from acting as their own general contractors.
- Will require an extensive amount of time to organize and supervise.

- Finding the best subcontractors can be time-consuming and costly.
- Might be difficult to juggle all the various aspects that require your attention.
- You will be liable for any potential injuries during the building process.

Pointers to Consider When You are Looking for Contractors

Hiring the perfect team for the job can be difficult if you're not exactly sure of how to go about it. Fortunately, we've got a few tips that will make the process a whole lot easier.

Reference Checks

The first step is always to perform reference checks. And never do just one. The contractor might hand you a few names of people you can do references with. In addition to checking those references, it's always a good idea to do some of your own checks.

Some valuable tips here include:

- Visit the barndos they have worked on. This will give you an idea of the quality of work to expect.
- Speak to the owners or residents about the quality of work, attention to detail as well as their ability to stick to scheduled deadlines.

- Contact the Better Business Bureau at http://www.bbb.org to confirm if the contractor is certified. Here you'll also be able to establish if there has been any negative feedback about work done.

- Use Google to check business reviews left by previous customers. Do this by typing in "business review (company name) (your city). This should give you details of reviews left on sites other than the company's official website.

Compare Bids, Quotes and Estimates

If there's one serious piece of advice, we'd like to impart to you, it's that you ALWAYS get more than one quote or estimate. Never settle on the first quote without comparing it to others in the area.

If you receive a quote that's considerably lower than all the others, always ask why. There might be hidden costs you aren't aware of. The last thing you need is a massive invoice halfway through the project when the budget has already been assigned.

Always Perform Face-to-Face Interviews

While it's convenient to do everything online, there are still some things that should always be done in person. Interviewing your potential barndo contractors is one of these things.

Having a face-to-face meeting with potential contractors will give you a gut feeling about the person as well as the work they're proposing to do. During the interview be sure to enquire about the easiest and most difficult barndo projects they've undertaken. That will give you an idea of how they'd be able to cope.

It's also crucial to be vigilant of contractors with little or no barndo-building experience. While these contractors may offer cheaper quotes, you might end up with considerably more costs in the long run when work needs to be redone.

Establish Subcontractors

If you're interviewing a potential general contractor, be sure to enquire about their connections to subcontractors. You will need a person who has worked with the type of people you need for your project.

More importantly, they need to have barndo-building experience. A general contractor with an established network of subcontractors will make your search process so much easier.

Insist on Contracts

Once you have identified a potential contractor, it's always recommended to draw up detailed contracts. A concise contract should have the following information:

- Start and completion dates.

- All costs—including admin fees (for documentation) and any other "hidden cost".
- A detailed payment schedule.
- Precise working hours, with agreed stipulations for weekends.
- List of materials to be used as well as who is responsible for supplying what and when.
- Material and workmanship guarantees.
- Insist on a "broom clause" where the contractor is obligated to leave a clean work site after work is completed.

Pro tip: *Never sign off on a contractor's work unless the relevant site inspections (as required by local regulations) have been done and passed and documentation received. If a plumber or electrician has to come back to fix an aspect that didn't pass inspection, they may charge it as a separate job if you signed off on the original job.*

Where to Find Contractors with Barndominium Experience?

If you're not in the building or construction business, it can be quite a task to sit down and start searching for contractors. Especially since a simple online search will reveal plenty of seemingly experienced contractors just waiting to give you the barndo of your dreams. The good news is that with a few tips, the search and subsequent streamlining process doesn't have to be a nightmare.

Consider the following:

- Use Google to search contractors in your area—create a list of everyone with a general 4-star rating and up and start checking their online referrals, experience and references.
- Join Facebook barndominium groups in your area and ask for references and suggestions.
- Speak to other barndo owners in the area—this might involve you knocking on a few strange doors, but in the end, having fellow barndo owners to talk to about your journey will be very helpful.
- Check for referrals from local barndo kit companies and hardware suppliers—if a contractor is well known to them, they may be able to give you a referral.

Key Takeaways

Before you start your barndo project, consider the following key takeaways:

- Establish if you're going to be your own general contractor or if you'll be hiring one.
- If possible, opt for companies that offer inclusive packages—that means they supply you with the

materials (barndo kit) as well as access to an expert team.

- If you're hiring your own team, be sure to check references and barndo-building experience.
- Never be too eager to accept a quote that is considerably lower than everyone else's it may be low for a bad reason.
- Always do additional research before opting for a specific contractor.
- Compare quotes, costs and timelines.
- Insist on a written contract detailing all the specifics.
- Never sign off on work unless it has passed inspection and necessary documents have been received.
- Consider all the pros and cons of being your own general contractor—it may not be easy, but it's not impossible!

Chapter 6: Drafting Floor Plans

Admit it. You've been envisioning a host of different designs and replaying different floor plans in your mind since you first thought about exploring the barndominium concept. You're not alone.

When we decided to stop dreaming about barndos and actually start building them, one of the most exciting aspects of the whole process was definitely the designing part of it all. The thought of finally having space to do exactly what we wanted to do was incredibly appealing to us.

What's more, with our specialized interest in small-scale design and architecture, we knew exactly what was possible and how to create it. Imagine our excitement! Fortunately, you don't have to be a home designer to create the perfect barndominium floor plan.

Floor plans can easily be obtained from a bunch of different sources. The trick is to have an idea of what you want. That includes knowing what house style you want, how many stories you want and of course how you want the interior to look and function. To help you figure it out, we'll be looking at the most common housing types and floor plans to consider.

Different Home Styles

Creating a barndominium is all about designing and creating the home of your dreams. That usually starts with the type of house style you want. Whether you're a minimalist, love the industrial look, want something shiny and modern or prefer a rustic farmhouse vibe, the good news is that there's a barndo design with your name on it. If you're unsure what your preferred home style is, we've added a list that should help you figure it out.

Modern

In a barndominium styled in a modern design, you're looking at a space where functionality meets style. Modern furnishings are sleek, boldly colored and often made of metal and glass. This is not the space for heavy wooden furniture.

Industrial

Barndos' built-in industrial style predominantly features steel elements and are essentially an extension of the steel exterior. Steel and wood accents create a clean, office-type look with little to no bright colors, ornaments or cushions and drapes.

Minimalist

There are many benefits to building your own barndo. One of them is that it's ideal for anyone preferring a minimalistic look or style. Since minimalistic styles require open space with very little furnishings and absolutely no clutter, it's quite easy to pull off with your barndo design.

Farmhouse

It's no secret that the farmhouse style is the most popular choice for barndo builders. This may be because it resonates with a country style or because it makes the thought of living in a barn-type home seem more appealing. With a farmhouse style, you're looking at large, traditional wooden accents. Heavy wooden furniture, warm rugs and even rustic kitchen decor.

Traditional Style

A traditional style is similar to the farmhouse design. Curtains instead of blinds, rugs on melamine floors and traditional furniture. Interior colors are rich and warm such as shades of burgundy, navy and even hunter's green.

Beach Style

Who doesn't enjoy a holiday home at the beach? To achieve this, you can do one of two things. Either build a barndo on or near a beach (if you can get the zoning permits) or simply create your own beach paradise anywhere you want.

The good news is that many companies offering floor plans have beach options available. For the interior, you're looking at bold, warm colors, seashell and beach-like decor and wide-open windows.

Just a Side Note...

When it comes to choosing a house style, there's no wrong or right. There's also no reason why you shouldn't mix different styles if that's your preference. After all, it's your home. We would like to highlight something that you might not have given much thought to. Just because you're building a barn doesn't mean it needs to *look* like a barn.

Different exterior finishes such as wood and stone can be added to create the outdoor style you want. For instance, it's very easy to cover your steel exterior with enough wooden accents to create a farmhouse barndo! That way you're giving yourself the best of both worlds—the pros of a steel frame with the design style of poles.

Floor Plan Types

Once you've identified your preferred style, it's time to decide on factors such as open plan, number of stories, and where everything is going to fit in your space. Here are some options to consider.

Open Plan Concept

Open plans are the most common floor plan ideas for barndos. In an open plan concept, there are very few walls. In fact, areas such as the living room, dining area and kitchen usually have no walls between them.

Walls are only used in sections of the home where privacy is required such as bedrooms and bathrooms. Creating this type of plan allows for better use of the space, and is considerably more cost-effective since there's no need to build walls or the foundations they need to stand on.

An open plan can also be aesthetically pleasing and create a certain flow to your home that's functional without being cluttered and restricted. Ordinarily, areas such as the living room, dining area and kitchen flow into each other. Offices, studies, bedrooms and bathrooms are placed toward the back of the barndo, away from the areas where you could have guests.

Creating a Business or Additional Living Area

For some people, opting for the barndo concept is about co-living with another family member such as parents-in-law or siblings. In this instance, you want a floor plan that divides the barndo into the required sections. If you'd prefer to not share communal areas, your builder can create a drywall to separate the two living areas.

This is also an ideal option if your business is in the same space as your living area. Here you'll select a floor plan with the necessary divisions to keep customers or employees from wandering into your private space.

What it boils down to there's a floor plan for your individual requirements. In some cases, you might need to have plans drawn up if the standard options don't work for you. Remember to add this to your budget.

Drafting Your Dream Layout

Now that we have discussed a little on floor plan types and uses, let's put that into action! At this point you will need to grab a pencil and paper. For this first part, all you will need to do is simply draw bubbles for each room. Once you have this done, look at it and make any changes needed.

Before we continue, it's important to go over some important tips. Read through these quick tips and again, make any changes required.

- Make sure you plan in enough storage space!
- Consider walking paths, no one wants to be tripping over things just to get a glass of milk.
- Ensure accurate assumptions for how much furniture you plan to have in your barndo.
- Safety for your children. Do their bedrooms need to be close to yours? Do they need to be on the second floor?

- Most importantly, will there be enough space for your dogs to play fetch and get their zoomies out?

Next, get the tape measure out and start measuring your current house or apartment. Measure the spaces you love and the spaces you don't. This will give you some easy mental notes on how big to measure out your barndo on paper.

Now you have a bubble draft of your barndo, and you have some rough room sizes in your head. Next, you will need either some graph paper or regular paper and a ruler. For your graph paper, come up with a ratio for the squares to feet, most likely 2 feet per square will suffice. If you are using the ruler, ¼ inch is the size of one square on the graph paper.

It's finally time to get those ideas down on that graph paper. Referencing your bubble layout, start measuring out and drawing your floor plans on the graph paper. Don't worry, this won't be your final draft, so it's ok to be messy still. Once you finish this, again, review it and make edits if wanted.

If you haven't already, now begin adding where you would like doors and the direction they should swing, window placements, and maybe appliance placements. You can feel free to add some furniture here, just be sure to measure them and draw them the correct size on the paper.

Just like that, you now have a rough draft of what you want your barndo layout to be! One of our most favorite parts was when we took our layout plans to be made into a 3d model so we could actually see what we were building! I highly recommend having a 3d version of your floor plans to be made on the computer if the architect or floor layout company doesn't do that for you.

Where to Get Floor Plans

Your next step is to speak to a company that specializes in floor plans to provide or create your required specifications. If you struggled just now trying to draw a rough floor plan layout, maybe you need to see more layouts to get inspiration from.

Here's a list of possible options to help you find the ideal floor plan at an affordable price.

- Start with popular companies in the area you're building—a simple Google search of "Barndominium floor plans (enter your area name)" should provide you with some options.
- Join social media groups for barndominiums in your area and ask the group where the best places to get floor plans are.
- Looking on Pinterest is a great place to find some really neat ideas.

- Speak to local barndo builders in the area (if you haven't chosen your builder yet, this might be a good time to start shortlisting options).
- Approach other barndo owners in the area and make some general inquiries.

As usual, we're not going to leave you hanging. We've compiled a list of some potential floor plan companies that may be worth a call. Before we get to that though, we need to share an important pro tip.

***Pro tip**: As eager as you may be to get your barndo built-in motion, it's crucial to contact a few floor plan companies. Never settle for the first option you find. Compare prices, and customer reviews and be sure to read the fine print before you agree to anything.*

Potential Floor Plan Companies to Consider

Here is a list of potential floor plan companies you can add to your shortlist.

1. **HOUSEPLANS**: This is a company with an extensive online catalog. They offer floor plans for a variety of styles and have single and double-story plans. There are 1 to 5+ bedroom options and include office shop and mother-in-law options. Additionally, there are also plans for garages, cottages and wrap-around porches. They deliver in all major regional areas such as Texas, Alabama,

Virginia, Tennessee and California. They're available at www.houseplans.com

2. **Architectural Designs:** If you're looking for a wide variety of options, this website boasts 175+ plans to choose from. Styles are varied with customizable options. You can find them on architecturaldesigns.com

3. **2dhouseplan:** While this website isn't as detailed as the previous two options, they do boast houses in two major categories. 25 Feet and 30 Feet options. Each category then has a few smaller options to browse through. They're at 2dhouseplan.com

4. **Texas Barndominiums:** This Texas company features several floor plans of different sizes and styles. They also offer building services. With this company, you have an option of choosing a floor plan from one of their previous builds or having a new one drawn up. But you'll have to use their designer. If you want to check them out, you can find them at texasbarndminium.com

Outdoor Entertainment Options

Very few barndominiums are built-in small, cramped areas. That said, you're most likely going to have a lot of open space at your disposal. Even after creating a designated space for your business, shop or workshop, garage, animal area and enormous play area for the kids, you may still have significant space to use.

If you're an outdoor person who enjoys time outside as much as we do, then your extra space can be well utilized as an outdoor entertainment area. If that's your current train of thought, you have several amazing options to consider.

Create a Pool Area

If you're in a warm climate that sees hot, sunny summers, a pool is always a good idea. With the ample space around your barndo, it could be easy to create a fenced-in pool area with all the bells and whistles to keep everyone cool and entertained.

Build a Wrap-Around Porch

Another fun and aesthetically pleasing feature is a wrap-around porch around your whole barndo. It's a stylish way to separate the front door from the walkway. It's also an ideal place to add some chairs or benches to enjoy the night air or even stargaze. Your builder will be able to advise you on the types and styles of porches or patios to build around your barndo.

Entertainment Area

Since barndos are considerably sizeable, you may want to opt for an indoor entertainment area that overflows to the outside. Creating a separate entertainment space is an excellent way to keep guests out of your living area.

By using awnings and outdoor blinds you can easily create the perfect space to barbeque or enjoy an al fresco dinner with the family or neighbors. If you're running your business from your barndo, this outdoor area could be the ideal spot to liaise and entertain potential clients!

Barndominium Landscaping Tips

Creating a lavish garden and outdoor area around your barndominium is just another way of enhancing the overall property. If you have children and pets, you'll also want to create a safe and fun play area for them. However, given the unusual shapes of many barndos, homeowners often find it challenging to create the perfect garden area.

Since most barndominiums are built on rural land, the good news is that you have considerably more space to create the perfect garden area. As you start creating your dream barndo, we've included a few landscaping tips to consider.

Assess the Climate

Before you start buying shrubs, trees or plants, it's crucial to consider the climate in your area. Regions that experience a lot of rainfall may need additional or specialized irrigation systems put in place to avoid flooding or soil erosion.

This is the same for the plants that you want to grow around your barndo. Always opt for native plants that can handle the natural temperature and rain conditions of the area.

Work According to Your Yard Size

If you're a gardening enthusiast, you might be delighted by the thought of such a large space to work with. On the other hand, having a large space can be overwhelming if it's your first garden. Some simple tricks for making the best of your yard size include:

- Divide the garden area into different sections such as a play area, garden, outdoor entertaining area and vegetable garden.
- Use potted plants or smaller fences to divide each section.
- If you have dogs, it might be a good idea to create a fence around our barndo to keep them from running into the road or land behind your property.

Create a Landscaping Design

As with your new dream home, it's important to create a design for your outdoor area. Decide upfront whether you will be adding additional trees and shrubs. An important point to consider here is to not plant trees with long roots close to your plumbing pipes, as this can become a problem down the line. Extensive root systems can easily block or become entangled with smaller plumbing pipes.

Add Stone Pathways and Solar Garden Lights

Every landscape feature needs a few beautifully constructed pathways between garden sections or even from the home to the driveway. Solar garden lights are a cost-effective way to light up the garden without pushing up your energy bill.

Make Your Barndo More Energy-Efficient

One of the questions we get asked a lot is, “How can I make my barndo more energy-efficient?” And with good reason. Due to the sheer size of some barndos, the average energy bill can be astronomical. If you’re running a business on the premises, this can add volumes to the cost. Ultimately, your dream barndo will be nothing more than an energy drain.

Additionally, the bulk of barndos are made from steel and it’s no secret that metal isn’t a good insulator, making it difficult to keep warm or cool. Aside from a huge energy bill, the last thing you want is an uncomfortable dream home. With that said, there’s some good news at the end of this cold tunnel.

Courtesy of modern technology, there are several effective ways to create or improve your barndos energy efficiency. It’s crucial to place your barndos energy efficiency at the top of your list and incorporate it into the initial build. This will be a lot cheaper than going back and trying to add it afterward. Let's take a look at the top ways to conserve energy in your dream barndo.

Building Orientation

Building orientation is an energy-conserving factor that you need to consider before you even start building. It refers to placing your building in the best possible direction to maximize the amount of heat absorbed during warmer and cooler months. Whether you'll be adding solar panels or not, it's always a good idea to place your barndo in the best direction to maximize the positives of your surroundings.

Opt For an Open Plan and Exposed Ceilings

If you're serious about energy efficiency, then choosing an open-concept floor design is the way to go. By minimizing the use of walls, you'll be promoting more air circulation. Additionally, exposed ceilings make it easier for your AC or furnace to heat or cool a room without being constricted by walls.

Single-Story Structures

Huge two-story barndos may look beautiful in the images you've been researching but it's important to understand that a bigger barndo is harder to keep warm or cool. Since heat rises, it's considerably easier to cool a single-story barndo. If you're opting for the two-story design, you should consider adding as many energy-saving features as possible to offset the cost of your energy bill.

Quality Insulation

The number one way to increase energy efficiency during the building process is to add quality insulation. Since barndos have deep wall cavities which are no good for keeping the air in or out. As a result, you'll have hot air escaping and cold air coming in.

When it comes to insulation, there are several choices to consider.

- **Blanket Insulation**: This is the standard insulation included in various types of homes. While the blankets are added to the walls and ceilings, this type of insulation offers the least insulating qualities. Building experts agree, this option shouldn't be a consideration for barndominiums.

- **Fiberglass Boards:** Rigid or fiberglass boards are used in spaces where it isn't always easy to add blown-in insulation or spray foam. Choosing this option means you can add fiberglass boards underneath the roof to minimize heat loss.

- **Spray Foam:** This is the option most recommended by barndo building experts, and we couldn't agree more. It works by expanding into any open crevasses in the wall cavity. Furthermore, it's excellent for crawlspaces and attics as it easily settles into the open spaces where you spray it. Some kit suppliers often include spray foam in their standard prefab kits.

Radiant Floor Heating

While insulating your walls and ceilings keeps air from seeping in through the roof and walls, what are you doing about the cold concrete slab under your floor? That's where radiant floor heating or RFH, comes in. Essentially, radiant floor heating refers to installing water-heated tubing under your barndos floors. Alternatively, this can also be achieved by using electric heating coils.

Adding an RFH system warms the space by radiating heat up from the floor. It's worth pointing out that an RFH system is more economical than regular heat furnaces. According to the U.S. Department of Energy, an effective RFH system can reduce your heating costs by up to 50 percent. That type of saving alone is reason enough to consider adding it to your barndo.

Energy-Efficient Windows and Doors

Commonly referred to as energy-saving windows and doors, these options are designed to prevent warm air from escaping through the windows. It works because these windows and doors boast increased insulation.

As the extra insulation keeps warm air in and cold air out, your space is automatically more comfortable, dramatically reducing the need to keep heating or cooling systems on all day. Do we need to emphasize that keeping heating and cooling systems off will reduce your energy bill even more?

To know whether or not your windows and doors are energy-efficient, simply look for the Energy Star logo. Designed to trap warm air, these windows are double or triple-pane and boast lower UV factors.

Energy-Efficient Plumbing

Another factor to consider before you even start the building and buying process is the addition of energy-efficient plumbing fixtures. Primarily, energy-efficient or green plumbing refers to using less power and less water to run your barndo. Some of the top ways to do this include the following:

- **Low-Flow Toilets:** These are toilets that function and perform similarly to regular toilets but are 20 percent more energy-efficient. It simply works by reducing the standard 1.6 gallons per flush of a standard toilet to the decreased amount of 1.3 gallons per flush. In comparison, older toilets use a whopping 8 gallons of water!
- **Low-Flow Shower Heads:** One of the most economical ways to save water is to add low-flow

shower heads to your barndo bathrooms. Essentially, you'll be using less water at an increased pressure to provide a decent shower.

- **Solar Water Heater:** If you're going to add solar panels to your barndo to save on electrical costs, it makes sense to switch from a regular water heater to a solar heater. Instead of relying on natural gas to warm up your water, you'll be relying on solar energy. Not only are cells cheaper but they're also more efficient.

Opt For a Range of Energy-Efficient Appliances

As you're dreaming of and designing your dream barndo, you've no doubt started giving thought to the types of furnishings and appliances you'd like to add. Considering energy-efficient appliances will not create a touch of style in your space but will also save you money.

Shopping for the most energy-efficient appliances for our barndo was quite a mission for us as we didn't really know what we were looking for. But, after some extensive legwork, this is what we found.

Fortunately, every appliance you'll need can be found in an energy-efficient version. That said, how are they different? For starters, basic home appliances such as washers, dryers, dishwashers and refrigerators make up about 20 percent of the average home's electric bill.

Switching to a more energy-efficient model will greatly reduce that amount.

It's as simple as looking through the appliance range from ENERGY STAR. These appliances are certified by the U.S. Department of Energy and have a lifespan of between 10 and 20 years. Be sure to enquire about the potential state or utility rebates associated with these products.

Pro tip: *On your first consultation with your building team, electricians and plumbers request a quote for fixtures and fittings that are more energy efficient. That way it will be easier to incorporate these products into your budget.*

One Story vs. Two Story

Depending on the amount of floor space you require, you might be thinking of adding a second story to your barndo. In fact, some barndo builders even opt to build their living space on top of an extended garage or animal housing section.

Alternatively, if you're running a business from your barndo you might opt to separate it from your living area by adding a whole separate floor for it rather than making the spaces side by side.

Cost Comparison

How does the cost of a two story barndo compare to that of a regular one story? On average, the price per square foot of a standard barndo varies between $35 and $175. A more exact cost will be determined by the materials, fittings, labor costs and kit style that you choose.

For the most part, a standard barndo usually ranges around the $150,000 mark. Of course, it all depends on the type of kit you're buying as well as the building team you're using.

Pros of Two Story

- Two story barndos are cheaper than standard two-story houses.
- An excellent advantage of the space as you're getting double the square footage for less.
- There's no need to increase the size of the foundation to create more space.
- Opting for a two-story building kit won't increase your estimated build time.
- Additional space can be used to create animal housing, space for business or even a garage.

Cons of Two Story

- Certain areas may have zoning restrictions on a two-story structure.
- Taller metal buildings might lack curb appeal and could end up looking more industrial.

- Installation of stairs or an elevator can be costly.
- Will require additional insulation and heating or cooling between the floors.
- Additional utilities will have to be installed.

Permits

One of the biggest hiccups we encountered on our barndo building journey was securing the right permits for the job. It's crucial to note that these permits vary from state to state and even city to city. What works in Alabama may not necessarily work in Virginia or Texas.

The first thing to do is find out exactly what's needed for the county or region you're going to build in. Here are a few more important pointers to consider when you're dealing with permits.

- All new builds and remodels will require a permit of some sort (this will include refurbishing your old barn).
- If you're demolishing an old house on your new property, you'll have to get a permit for the barndo you're building in its place.
- Some permits come with special instructions to protect properties in built-in areas prone to severe weather disasters such as hurricanes or tornadoes.

- Building without the necessary will result in severe penalties and fines.
- All types of building permits can be obtained from the local government agency that grants building permits if you're new to the area, speak to someone who knows!
- Building plans will be reviewed and authorized if compliant—never start building without the permit.
- The cost of a permit depends on the area you want to build on and the type of plans, but the national average is $1,380.
- The time you have to wait for a permit can vary from one day to two weeks.
- Anyone involved in your project can pull the permits necessary for the build—if you're using a contractor, they will most likely do it for you double check this before any work starts.
- To apply for your permit, you'll need a copy of the barndo building plans.

Key Takeaways

Some of the crucial takeaways from this chapter include the following:

- Identify your preferred house style to get the design process started.
- Opt for a reputable company or architect to provide you with floor plans.
- Design the landscaping for the area around your barndo—it will create a stylish outdoor area and approve your curb appeal.
- Be sure to incorporate a few of our energy-efficient tips into your barndo build to create a comfortable barndominium.
- Review the pros and cons of a two-story build before deciding on that option.
- Ensure you (or your builder) obtain the correct permits necessary.
- Be sure to hold off starting any building until the permits are in place.

With floor plans and permits in place, it's time to decide whether you'd prefer to use a prefab kit or do a custom build. Keep reading to see which you prefer.

Chapter 7: Custom Plans Versus Kits

Do you have a plan in mind of how you want your barndo to look? Once you've decided on the ideal location for your dream barndo, the next two major decisions you need to make are:

- Steel or pole?
- Custom plan or kit?

This chapter takes an in-depth look at the differences between custom plans vs. kits. Understanding how each option stacks up will make it so much easier to select a choice that suits your budget and your design style. We'll also give you a breakdown of the pros and cons of both steel structures and pole barns.

While you might already have an idea of what you want your barndo to look like, it's important to understand the pros and cons of each option. This section is especially helpful to barndo dreamers who really aren't sure about the major differences between each option.

Barndo Transformation

You might find yourself in a position where you already own property with an existing barn on it. Granted, it most probably doesn't look quite like the barndominium images you've been Googling for days on end.

It might still, however, leave you wondering if you can transform an old, not-so-shoddy barn into a luxury barndominium. The good news is that you can!

How Do You Turn Existing Barns into Barndos?

If you already own a property with a barn on it, it might seem like a more affordable option to just convert the one you already have. To some extent that may be true. However, it mostly comes down to the age and condition of the structure you're starting with.

One of the biggest advantages of already having a barn is that you most likely own the land so there's no need to find financing to purchase the land at the beginning of your project. Let's take a look at a few other pros and cons of refurbishing a pre-existing barn.

Pros of Refurbishing

- Refurbishing an existing barn can be cheaper if the original structure is in very good condition.
- Minor renovations will be faster to perform than building from scratch.
- Repurposing your old barn provides you with a more sustainable option and less wasted material.

- It's almost a given that your existing structure already has the necessary permits and meets any zoning requirements.

Cons of Refurbishing

- Very little room for customization as you'll pretty much be stuck with the general design of the original structure.
- Renovations such as insulation can be costly if it didn't exist in the structure before.

Building From Scratch

For us personally, there was never any doubt that we would build our barndo from scratch. Yes, it meant months of more work, much more research, and probably ten times more interaction between us and our team of contractors, but in the end, it was worth it.

The reason is that building from scratch offers you one golden nugget that refurbishing never can—**total control of every inch of the customization factor**. If, like us, you want large open plan designs that allow you to merge spaces uniquely and stylishly, then you'll never consider any other option.

However, as fun as starting with a blank canvas can be, there are a few downsides. We'd like to share a few of the pros and cons we encountered along the way.

Pros of Building from Scratch

- The customization factor—you can design your house EXACTLY the way you envision.
- You're not stuck with pre-existing issues in an older building.
- You can easily incorporate another kit onto your new building to create your business.

Cons of Building from Scratch

- Clearing the vegetation and trees on a newly bought property can be expensive and time-consuming.
- Customization options can also become costly—more lavish spaces come with bigger price tags.
- Zoning regulations and permits need to be obtained on a new structure, depending on your location this can be time consuming and restricting.

Custom Plans vs. Kits

If you've made the decision to build from scratch, your next decision centers around choosing a custom plan or a pre-designed kit. As the name suggests, a custom plan is quite simply a plan that you or your architect design based on your requirements and the space available. A kit, on the other hand, is a steel frame available in predetermined sizes.

Barndominium Kits

Many first-time barndo builders often opt for a kit because it's cheaper and in some cases easier to build. This is mostly because there are no elaborate architectural designs and luxury materials needed as might be the case when you're drawing up a custom plan.

Since the frame is pre-designed and created to certain specifications, construction time is considerably shorter. Kits are also perfect if you're not too finicky over the customization factor.

Essentially, what you get with your barndo kit might vary slightly depending on the company you're purchasing it from. However, it's been our experience that most reputable companies offer a fairly standard package. The most common packages include the following:

- Barndominium shell (or frame)
- Concrete slab that serves as your foundation
- Concrete floors
- Exterior doors
- Windows (many companies offer energy-efficient options)

- Spray foam insulation that ensures your frame fits snugly together and keeps heat in
- A standard roof

We should stress though that it's important to do your research on what different companies offer. Thorough research may lead you to a company that offers a few extras for a similar price as competitors offering less. Be sure to ask for sample photos of how the interior and exterior of each kit will look. Compare actual sizes to your expectations.

Pros of Kits

- Prefabricated kits are cost-effective and usually range from $20 to $140 per square foot.
- Shorter construction time.
- Kits are all constructed using galvanized steel, so you're assured of durability.
- Additional kits can easily be added to your existing kit to expand your home (our children always refer to prefab kits as Legos for grownups!).
- Prefab kits are easy to insulate as they're designed to fit together with minimal heat loss.
- Since kits are built to exact specifications there's very little waste, making this an eco-friendlier option.

Cons of Kits

- Fewer customizable options.
- Using a standardized template means your home isn't as unique as you'd like.
- Most styles feature a modern look which isn't ideal if you're looking for a more traditional looking home (adding the stone or wood paneling to create a traditional look can be costly).
- Obtaining certain zoning regulations can be challenging as the prefab structures don't follow a traditional home design.

Costing Associated with Prefab Kits

Despite kits being standardized, there's still not really a "one-size-fits-all" price tag for your barndo. Factors such as materials, interior, types and quantities of doors and foundations all play a part in determining the eventual cost.

That said, Green Building Elements recently published an article summarizing the costing structure quite effectively. This is how they summarized it.

Factors To Price	Estimated Costs
DIY barndominium shell/frame	$22 per sq. ft
High-end barndominium shell/frame	$140 per sq. ft
Average cost	$70 per sq. ft
Delivery	Usually 10%
Windows & doors	20%
6" foundation	$5 per sq. ft
Fittings	$20-80 per sq. ft
Construction	$2-4 per sq. ft

While these are just average amounts and various factors that will determine what your actual costs are, it gives you a general guide to work with when you consider a prefab kit.

Websites You Can Check Out for Barndo Kit Options

The good news is that many companies all over America offer a variety of barndominium kits at varying prices. Many of these companies offer nationwide delivery, making it easy to choose the option that best suits your style and budget. Keep in mind though that delivery charges will apply and could become quite costly if the chosen company is far from your location.

We've listed some of the more common barndo kit suppliers to give your search a jump start.

1. Maverick Steel Buildings Inc.
2. Timberlyne.
3. Green Building Elements.
4. General Steel Buildings.
5. SteelCo Building.
6. Metal Depots.
7. Worldwide Steel Buildings.
8. Absolute Steel Texas.

9. Sunward Steel Buildings.

10. Heritage Buildings.

11. DC Builders.

12. Barn Pros Nationwide.

13. Beehive Buildings.

Custom Plans

As we've mentioned before if you're a stickler for the customization factor, and your budget allows, creating a custom plan can be both rewarding and fun. In short, you have a lot more control over every aspect of your dream living space.

How many times have you heard someone say, "I wish this was different" or "It would have been nicer if this was different about my home"? Well, when you're creating your own space, you don't have those issues.

If you're going to work with an architect or a designer, they may even be able to create 3D templates of the images you have in mind. That way you'll be able to make alterations before any work begins.

It's important to note that custom plans are often considerably more expensive than prefab plans because you're creating everything from the exterior to the types of walls, ceilings, windows, doors and more. Once your design is approved, it's sent to the manufacturer to be created.

Pros of Custom Plans

- Ideal for barndo dreamers who want to customize every aspect of their living space.
- You can create a truly unique home or home-business combo.
- Designs can easily incorporate various materials such as wood and stone to create a more traditional look over your steel frames.

Cons of Custom Plans

- Necessities such as wiring, plumbing, heating and insulation can become quite expensive on an elaborate custom plan.
- Combining materials can be costly and may delay the building process.
- Might have to consult with an architect or designer to create a practical rendering.

Cost of Custom Plans

It's difficult to determine a ballpark cost for a custom plan. Frankly because of the many variables. Factors such as size, material, interior design, size and style of windows and doors.

Pole Barn vs. Steel Structure

When it comes to deciding on the material you can construct your barndo out of, you usually only have two choices. Pole barn or steel structure. As far as similarities go, they both share the basic barndo fundamentals such as large frames with posts spaced eight feet or more apart. What is the difference and is one better than the other?

Pole Barn

Essentially, a pole barndo has a wood post-frame construction. Picture the traditional barns on the homesteads of old and you have the basic idea of a pole barn. Wood posts are anchored into the ground and form the basic frame.

For the most part, the pole posts are spaced between 8 and 12 feet apart. Most builders will recommend that pole posts be spaced closer together since they don't offer as much support as a steel structure.

Opting for a pole barn design doesn't limit your design options and you just as easily have an open plan design or a more traditional structure. As with any building structure, pole barns do have their pros and cons and it's crucial to look into these as you shortlist your options.

Pros of Pole Barn

- Pole barns are rust-resistant.

- The construction process is quicker and with the right team you can even erect it in a few days as there's often no need for a foundation.
- Construction costs are generally lower, ranging between $15 to $35 per square foot and labor costs are generally cheaper.

Cons of Pole Barn

- The wood frame can shift which may lead to drywall cracking.
- Over time the structural integrity of wood deteriorates.
- Many pole barn homes are susceptible to ground settling.
- Wood posts and studs may splinter or crack in severe weather.
- Pole homes are at risk of damage from termites which can weaken a structure within a few months.
- Humid climates can cause mold or bacteria to settle in the poles—treatment to combat this can be costly.
- Experts estimate that insurance can cost up to 40% more for pole structures.

- Fire can start burning wood at about 572 degrees Fahrenheit, making your pole barndo a huge fire risk.

While in this instance it may seem that the negatives outweigh the positives, it doesn't mean you can't have a pole barn frame for your dream barndo. It just means that you will have to factor in additional costs to have the wood specially treated. It also means that you will have to opt for a location that isn't exposed to unusually high levels of moisture or humidity.

Pro tip: *Never opt for a pole barn in an area prone to severe weather conditions. After all, one of the goals of building a barndo should be to have the strongest home possible. Always consider your surroundings.*

Steel Structure

Essentially, steel-structured barndos are more popular than their wooden counterparts and it's easy to see why. For starters, a steel frame is mounted onto a concrete foundation. Exterior walls are then made up of aluminum or metal sidings. The structure also features a metal roof.

While the frame is made up of thick steel columns that are usually spaced between 12 and 20 feet apart, making this an ideal option for large, spacious floor plans. Another factor that makes steel structures a more popular choice is that a steel frame creates superior support for rafters and roof beams, even in the windiest conditions. As with the pole barn option, we'll discuss the most significant pros and cons to consider.

Pros of Steel Structure

- Steel frames are durable and if maintained correctly can last for up to 100 years.
- These types of frames offer greater protection from severe weather elements, making them ideal for areas prone to hurricanes or tornadoes.
- Steel structures are also fire resistant and can withstand temperatures up to 2,500 degrees Fahrenheit.
- Due to the strength of the material, insurance costs are generally lower.
- Steel columns that are spaced further apart make large, open plan designs more possible.
- Despite having a slightly higher building cost varying between $15 and $35 per square foot, it's still cheaper than a standard house.
- Steel is also not prone to rot or termites.
- Since the columns are anchored to a concrete foundation, it means there's no shifting as the ground settles.

- Steel will also not warp in severe exposure to water and can withstand prolonged exposure to snow or rain.

Cons of Steel Structure

- Steel structures are prone to corrosion and rust caused by moisture and will need special treatment and insulation.
- Steel structures take longer to build as you need to wait for the foundation to settle before erecting the frame.
- While the cost is cheaper than a regular house, it's still more expensive than a pole barn frame.

Pro tip: *When opting for a steel structure, insist on your contractor using galvanized steel. Essentially, galvanized steel doesn't rust or corrode and will always be a more durable option than mild steel for instance. This is the one instance where you shouldn't opt for a shortcut.*

Key Takeaway

The key takeaways to consider when it comes to custom plans vs. kits are:

- Existing barns can be refurbished, depending on the condition of the structure—although it could be costly.

- Building from scratch, using a custom plan gives you complete control over the customization factor.

- Using prefab kits is considerably cheaper and easier and often a popular choice for first-time barndo builders.

- Looking at options for steel structures has many benefits which outweigh more traditional pole options.

- Most barndominium building kit suppliers deliver nationwide, making it easy to get the best kit at the best price delivered to the vacant property.

- Many barndo owners start with small to medium kits and as more funds become available, bigger kits can be purchased and added onto the existing barndo—it's an affordable way to build your barndo to your desired size over time.

Once you've decided on the material, custom plan, or prefab kit, the real fun begins. Arranging delivery and putting your dream together! At this point, you're closer to moving day than you realize.

Chapter 8: The Building Process

At this stage of your barndo-building journey, you should be feeling very excited! If you're finalizing your floor plan, it means you are almost ready to start the building process. And that in turn means that you are only a few weeks away from moving day. What could be more exciting?

When we reached this phase of our barndo dream, it was almost impossible to contain our excitement. Even our three precious golden retrievers were excited. They may have not known what we were all excited about, but we're sure they could sense something wonderful was about to happen. The kids, on the other hand, were excited by the thought of having bigger, more spacious rooms. And of course, the thought of all that outdoor space excited everyone tenfold!

By this stage, we had already started packing up the old house. The general consensus in our household was that the very minute our dream barndo was ready we'd be there, moving in and living the dream. Are you feeling this energy yet?

Finalizing Your Floor Plan and Adding the Final Considerations

It's crucial though to review your floor plan and check your final considerations for a few last-minute additions. If your budget seems to be on track with some room for extras, it might be a good idea to include a few of your *wants* that were only dreams in chapter two.

We've listed a few considerations you might want to give some thought to as you finalize your floor plan. This becomes more possible if you realize you have space in your budget.

Choosing the Best Direction for Maximum Sunlight

As you're getting ready to build your barndo, you might be looking at your open piece of land dreaming of your dream home. With that in mind, have you given any thought to the direction your home should be facing for maximum sunlight?

Essentially, your home should be facing north or northeast to receive the most direct sunlight during the day. This is especially beneficial in the winter months when the sun is at its lowest.

If you're planning to include solar panels to your roof during the build or at some point a north-facing home will maximize the sun your panels can absorb. Speak to your architect about this before finalizing the plans.

Enclosed Porch

Essentially, an enclosed porch refers to the space around your barndo. Covering this space with a roof and screened-in sides create a stylish space between the front door and the pathway. Since an enclosed porch has a screen, you and your family can enjoy the outdoors without being exposed to the weather elements. As an extension of your barndo, check with your contractor or architect that the addition is authorized under your current building permit.

Balcony

Usually, balconies are quite popular with barndo builders who have opted for a two-story home. Balconies are a wonderful way for the people upstairs to enjoy the outdoors without having to go downstairs and then outside. Many two-story barndo kits will already feature a balcony option.

If however, you're adding your balcony from scratch, as with the porch, be sure to check if you require additional permission on your permit. You can also choose between an uncovered balcony or opt for a covered version. Outdoor blinds make an excellent covering for balconies.

Types/Shapes of Windows to Consider

Not all barndo windows are created equally. Some are big and square while others are small and round. It all depends on what your individual preference is and how much budget you've allocated to windows. Several popular choices are firm favorites with barndo owners.

- **Bay Windows:** Generally, bay windows are placed to extend beyond the side of a building. Not only do they create the illusion of extra space, but they also let in additional light.

- **Picture Windows:** If you want to let in a lot of light, then picture windows are well worth considering. Picture windows are essentially designed to provide a large, unobstructed view of the outdoors, making them ideal choices for living rooms, dining rooms or even bedrooms.

- **Casement Windows:** One of the more popular options for barndos is casement windows because they offer superior ventilation and can easily be opened. Additionally, they're easy to clean and feature a tight seal to ensure they close properly.

- **Awning Windows:** Many people prefer awning windows because they are available in a variety of styles that can suit any barndo home decor and style. Additionally, awning windows open from the top, making it simple to open the window without insects flying in.

- **Sliding Windows:** Since sliding windows boast an amazingly tight seal, they're well-known for being energy efficient. They're also easy to clean and remarkably affordable.

- **Storm Windows:** Depending on how prevalent storms are in your area, it might be a good idea to opt for storm windows. Essentially, they add an extra layer of protection during storms and strong winds. More good news is that storm windows are relatively inexpensive and perfect for barndos!

While we have suggested opting for standard windows to minimize costs, there's no reason why you shouldn't consider a more elegant window choice if your budget allows it!

Skylights

If you haven't considered adding skylights up to this point, it's a good idea to add a few to your plans. Skylights are not only energy-efficient but are the perfect way to add natural light to your space.

Furthermore, skylights are an ideal way to bring light into spaces that may be darker than the rest of your barndo. We are of course referring to bathrooms, laundry rooms, kitchens and even hallways. Opting for traditional skylights, will need a direct line of sight to the outdoor light. More modern tubular skylights, on the other hand, can be configured around obstructions to provide light where it's needed.

Adding skylights in darker areas means you won't have to keep an artificial light on all the time. That in turn will save you a bunch of money on your energy bill.

Ceiling Heights

Another fun feature of barndominiums is that they can have ceilings designed to your unique decor style. Standard homes usually have ceiling heights that vary between 8 to 9 ft (2.4 to 2.7m). Barndos on the other hand can have stunning vaulted ceilings with heights of about 14 ft (4.3m) or more if you prefer.

Higher ceilings provide dimension, add extra natural light and essentially make your barndo seem more spacious. (Just in case it's not already spacious enough)

Adequate Space for Intended Amount of Occupants

One of the top reasons people switch to the barndominium lifestyle is the added space that you get. For us, it was an absolute blessing to move from a regular city house to a barndominium with a ton of added space.

That said, before finalizing your floor plan, you should make sure that there's adequate space for the number of people that will be living in your barndo. Ideally, it should be an opportunity to give each child (and dog if you want) their own bedroom.

If space allows, create that study or office you've always wanted. Essentially all the space issues you had in your current home should be resolved. Where possible, include a few guest rooms and bathrooms to make sleepovers a whole lot more fun.

Storage Space

On the note of space, it's equally important to create sufficient storage space. With the added space, each bedroom can be made slightly bigger to include additional cupboards or storage options. Having adequate storage is the key to keeping your barndo clutter-free!

Will You Include a Garage?

Depending on how big your barndo is, and what your plans are with the outdoors, you will most likely want to include a garage or two. If you have the space, create a garage big enough to easily house all your vehicles. You might want to include a few storage solutions as well, to keep the space tidy.

Some popular barndo kits offer a garage plan that boasts over 1,000 square feet on one side, and then a two or three-bay space on the right for two or three vehicles. It's also an ideal time to squeeze in that small DIY workshop you could never have in a smaller city home.

Design a Spacious Laundry Room

One of the rooms that people often neglect in their design process is the laundry room. Our recommendation is to make the laundry room slightly larger than you anticipated. Rather than creating a dingy little room in the back corner, opt for a space big enough to place a washer, dryer, sink and perhaps even a storage cupboard.

It may also be functional to add a few shelves. Generally, laundry rooms are often exposed to excess moisture and dampness. It's a good idea to add a window or two to provide sunlight and ventilation. If the space is excessively dark, consider a small skylight. Making your laundry room more efficient will go a long way to being more organized and who knows, doing the laundry might not seem like such a chore!

Create an Outdoor Living Space

If your family enjoys the outdoors as much as our family does, then an outdoor living space is an absolute must. Whether you set up a pool area, barbeque area or play area for the kids, having an outdoor space is a great addition to your barndo area.

The best part of an outdoor living area is that it can be upgraded as you go along. A simple barbeque area can evolve into a full-on outdoor entertainment area as funds become available.

Finalize Your Lot Selection (If Not Completed Yet)

If you're still finalizing your lot selection, it's important to keep a few considerations from Chapter 4 in mind.

- Choose the amenities you're prepared to live with and without—How close to the town/city do you need to be to still be comfortable?
- How important is spending time outdoors? This may leave you leaning toward a place that has a more picturesque landscape with opportunities for outdoor activities.
- Does the weather of a specific area appeal to you more than some of your other options?
- Have you considered the price differences between your favorite properties? How does each option affect your monthly repayment plan?
- Will some options on your shortlist be easier to build on in terms of land prep, zoning and permits?
- Have you reviewed the different tax implications of each potential property on your shortlist?
- How accessible are the options on your shortlist? How will this affect the cost of land prep and contractors getting on and off the property?

Waiting for Building Permits and Zoning

We've mentioned this before, but it's important enough to mention it again. No building work may be started on the property BEFORE the necessary permits have been obtained. Speak to your general contractor well in advance to draw up a schedule of which permits must be pulled and when. It really does work much quicker and simpler if the contractor pulls them for you.

Timeline for Permits

Obtaining the necessary permits may often take longer than you'd expect. Depending on where you live you might wait anywhere between **three to six weeks**. Any amendments you're required to make might add another two weeks to the process.

Furthermore, depending on the type of permit you've requested, you may only have a specified time to complete the project before the permit expires. Most general contractors make use of a pre-construction checklist that helps keep everything on track with the various permits.

Building Stages of Your Barndominium

There's nothing quite as exhilarating as showing up to your empty lot on the first day of building. Watching the builders arrive is a sure sign that building your dream barndo is about to get underway. Months of planning, running around, making thousands of phone calls, searching properties and calculating budgets have led you to this point. It's important to take a step back and breathe it all in because from here on out it's going to get a whole lot crazier!

Not sure what to expect? Fortunately, we've compiled a step-by-step list of the process and how it's most likely to go. You might already have discussed this with your builder or general contractor. Your building process should look something like this.

Plan the Work, Work the Plan

Remember the old adage, "Plan the work, work the plan," well truer words have never been spoken when it comes to setting out on your barndominium journey. It certainly rings true during the building stage of your barndominium.

We've seen barndo builders on the verge of going crazy or simply just quitting because everything seems so haphazard and chaotic. We really can't stress enough how important planning is and more importantly, how crucial it is to stick to the plan as best as you can. Always have a plan B for days when it may be raining, or other hiccups derail your daily schedule. The essential goal is to have everyone moving forward every day.

It should also go without saying that your general contractor should become your new best friend. This is the person who's going to get you moving forward when you're looking at your third straight day of rain and no real work.

That said, the average barndominium construction time takes about three to six months from start to finish. If you've opted for a smaller, simpler barndo kit that doesn't have too many bells and whistles, it may even be possible to get your dream barndo up in a matter of weeks.

To give you an idea of how the general flow of your building process will work, we've drawn up a bit of a flow chart to help you understand how the dream creation process is going to pan out. We've mentioned this before, but before we jump into the flow chart, we should reiterate the following—**Never take shortcuts or opt for sub-quality materials.** After all, you want a safe dream home. With that said, let's check out the flow chart.

Lot Preparation

Estimated Time: 7 Days

Nothing can happen unless the lot is cleared of vegetation and the land prepared. Ensure this gets done while you're waiting for supplies to be delivered. An unprepared lot can set you back by as much as a week, depending on what needs to be done on it.

A good way to ensure your lot prep is done on time is to clean and clear it as soon as the property is signed over to your name. You won't be able to start building until you've received the permits, but nothing stops you from cleaning your property!

Foundation

Estimated Time: 7-14 Days

For the most part, barndo foundations are built on concrete slabs. A shoddy foundation will cost you dearly in the long run, so it should be done properly the first time around. Essentially, your foundation will have to hold the barndo shell, your home contents and any vehicles you're going to keep in the barndo. Don't rush the process of building on your slab until it has dried.

According to the Concrete Network, concrete should be allowed to cure for about seven days before putting extensive weight on it. It's important to note that a thicker slab will take longer to dry. On average four to six inches of concrete slab takes about 26 days to reach its full strength. Your contractor will most likely advise you on the best option for your particular kit.

Framing and Structure

Estimated Time: 2-14 Days (depending on size)

If you've opted for a barndominium kit, this part actually goes very quickly. In fact, you might be surprised to learn that some of the simpler kits can easily be built with only two people. It's during this phase that windows and doors will be fitted to the completed frame.

HVAC, Plumbing and Electrical

Estimated Time: Plumbing: 3-5 Days

Electrical & HVAC: 3-5 Days

It's worth pointing out that plumbing in a barndo isn't done the same way as in a conventional home. When you're building a home in the city, plumbing pipes are built on traditional foundations that usually have crawl spaces.

On a barndo build, there are no foundations or crawl spaces. Instead, the pipes are laid into the concrete slabs which means plumbing needs to be done at the same time as the slab is laid. This makes it crucial to have your floor plan finalized before any concrete is laid to prevent any errors or last-minute changes. Once the plumbing pipes are laid, there's no turning back.

Once that's been completed, the electrical team will start laying cables, hooking up any wiring as well as installing power outlets. It's at this point that you need to advise the electrical guys if you need more outlets to ensure that the existing ones aren't overloaded.

You'd also want to point out any high-powered appliances that may require additional power or an individual circuit. Since barndos are open plan and don't have that many walls for power outlets, you might need to consider floor outlets. Another good idea is to place power outlets close to entrances. Most general contractors recommend having outlets no further than 12 feet apart because it just makes the electrical process so much easier for the homeowner. Floor outlets also need special coverings to minimize the risk of damage. Covers will also keep moisture from building up in your outlets.

When the electrical and plumbing guys are finished, the HVAC can be hooked up. Be sure to test everything before giving your seal of approval.

Insulation

Estimated Time: 2-3 Days (smaller barndos one to two days)

A few years back, when the barndo concept was new and fresh, insulation wasn't a prerequisite. Recent years have seen a change in building codes and insulation is now mandatory in all barndo structures. Your general contractor will advise you of the ideal insulation for your barndo, but as we've mentioned before, you can never go wrong with spray foam.

Drywall, Paint and Flooring

Estimated Time: Flooring: 2 Weeks

Drywall: 2-3 Days

Taping and Painting: 2-5 Days

Once the initial plumbing and electrical inspections have been done and passed, it's time to start hanging drywalls, painting interiors and laying floors. Generally, drywalling comes in 4 x 8-foot sheets and is usually installed horizontally. Given the sheer size of drywalling (especially for higher ceiling barndos), it's a good idea to have a professional handle this cumbersome task.

If you've opted to do the painting yourself, consider hiring a sprayer to make the painting go quicker. (This will still be cheaper than opting for a subcontractor to do it) Always do the flooring last to prevent any damages or paint spills to your new flooring.

Interior and Exterior Finishes

Estimated Time: 3-6 Weeks

At this stage of your barndo experience, you will be experiencing a crazed mixture of excitement, exhaustion and panic over what you think you may have missed. The good news is that if you've been sticking to the plan or a semblance of a plan, then you're closer to moving day than ever.

While the sub-contractors are completing their particular jobs, it's a good idea to get the whole family involved in helping with the last interior and exterior finishes. Interior work includes cabinetry, interior doors, countertops, fixtures and lighting. Exterior work may include walls, roof, doors and windows. Be sure to take several walks in and around your barndo during the days leading up to the end of the project. Have a notepad and pen handy to jot down anything that looks out of place.

Final Inspection and Walkthrough

The day of the final inspection will be the day that you're finally granted permission to move into your barndo. For this to happen the major essentials such as plumbing and electrical need to be 100 percent in working order. Be sure to test and double-check all power outlets and plumbing fixtures as part of your daily walkthroughs. Hold all subcontractors accountable for cleaning up after their teams. (Remember the broom clause of chapter five)

A few of the inspections to be aware of are listed below. Some may vary, depending on the state you're living in. Some states also refer to these documents by their official number, so we've included them, for your convenience.

- **Building Final (Document Number 925):** Done after all work is finalized. This is also referred to as the final inspection.
- **Electric Rough (Document Number 300):** Usually done after the installation of rough wiring and electrical boxes.
- **Electric Final:** Done once power is connected to the building and all electrical work as well as electrical trim has been installed.
- **Framing (Document Number 200):** Checked once all the construction is dried in. All necessary applications such as plumbing, electrical, mechanical and gas work should be completed,

and the relevant inspections are done. Insulation should NOT be installed prior to the inspection.

- **Roof Final (Document Number 955):** This inspection is done to ensure that the roof meets all zoning, building codes and safety regulations.
- **Zoning Final (Document Number 965):** Once the build is complete, a final zoning inspection will be done to ensure that all zoning requirements have been met.

Moving In

Moving day is stressful no matter where you're moving to. But there's something different about moving into *your own* barndominium. While the process has its stressful moments, moving day is what you've been working toward, so it's really a different kind of excitement that fills the air. It's the satisfaction that months, if not years of planning have finally come to fruition.

Common Time Delays During the Construction Process

No matter how well you plan your barndo-building plan, there's always the risk of delays. When this happens, it's important to stay positive! A delay in one of your processes doesn't mean the end of your dream, it merely means you have something else to sort out. If you've made it this far, a few more small delays shouldn't get you down.

Some of the more common delays you might encounter include the following:

- Delays with receiving permits or zoning permissions.
- Vendors and suppliers who don't have stock of required building supplies.
- Possible delays with material deliveries.
- Contractors who call in sick or don't have stock of what's needed to finalize a job.
- Kitchen cabinets are delivered in the wrong color or size.
- And, our personal favorite, bad weather halting the building process.

If you are faced with delays in one aspect of your project, focus your energy on another part of the journey. If it's raining for seven days in a row, use the time to pack and organize at the old house. Or if your budget permits, spare time can be used to shop for the interior knick-knacks that will make your barndo a home.

Alternatively, if there's a delivery delay of your supplies and materials, use the time to organize or design your landscaping. There's always something that needs to be done during the barndo adventure, so there's actually no excuse for idle hands!

Key Takeaways

As you prepare to finalize the last stages of your barndo project, consider these significant key takeaways:

- Assess the pros and cons of your shortlisted lot options.
- Finalize your plan before setting out to start the build as this affects aspects such as the plumbing and electrical placement.
- Obtain **ALL** necessary building and zoning permits before beginning any building work on the property. This means not doing anything that's covered by the permits you've applied for.
- Review final considerations such as porches, balconies, window types and skylight options.
- Consider what cosmetic additions you can make with money left in the budget—remember that changes to the structure affect zoning and building permit applications.
- Factor in space and storage for all individual occupants. Never forget to utilize your extra space to make everyone comfortable.
- Don't let delays hamper your dream or the progress of your barndominium.

Stay positive—You got this!

Conclusion: And Finally...

When we started this book, we had one real goal in mind. And that was to highlight and provide basic alternatives to the many hiccups on the journey to building your dream barndo. Wanting to live in a barndominium is one thing. Getting from your dream to moving day can be quite a challenge, especially if you're not sure where to start.

We hope our simple, yet informative guide has provided you with the inspiration needed to stop dreaming and start building. On that note, let's recap some of the more significant pointers you should consider as you embark on this fun and crazy journey.

First Things First. Before you start drawing up plans and buying materials, it's crucial to decide what function you want your barndo to serve. Will it simply be a spacious family home, or will you share the home with an extended family? You also have to determine if the extended family (such as parents-in-law) will stay in the actual barndo or if you'll build an extension onto your living area.

Alternatively, you might want to run a shop or other type of business from the same space. This will be a crucial factor in helping you decide on the type of plan to opt for and what will be needed. If you're still on the fence about whether you should or shouldn't invest in a barndominium, it might help to compare the pros and cons of building your own barndo. The two most significant pros have to be the highly customizable factor and the wide-open spaces.

To Refurbish, or Not. Deciding to create a barndominium can stem from already owning land with an old barn on it. Depending on the state of your property and the existing structure, this could be an excellent way to achieve your barndo dream without a lot of hassle. Already owning land or a barn will reduce the amount of financing you may need.

However, the one downside of refurbishing an existing barn is that your customizable factor might be very limited. You will have to work with an existing shape, size and ceiling height. It's up to you to decide if you can turn the existing barn into your dream barndominium. If the building is very dated, there will be additional costs to bring it up to code. This might include factors such as insulation, plumbing, and electrical.

Location! Location! We can't stress the importance of finding the perfect location. Unless you've already made up your mind, consider stepping out of your comfort zone as you review potential options. Furthermore, some states are cheaper with kit and barndo costs in general.

In some areas, your desired location might be too far from the local water and sewer main lines for a simple connection. In this instance, you will have to build your own systems. Unless your budget can accommodate this type of expense, this location might not be ideal. Zoning regulations in some areas are also more flexible, especially toward non-conventional builds. Review your family's needs versus what the potential environment can offer you.

Reach Out. When you've decided on the location, it's always a good idea to reach out to other barndominium owners in the area. Other than randomly knocking on strangers' doors, a more productive way is to join Facebook barndo groups in the area. Use these groups to interact with fellow owners, builders and even potential suppliers. Doing this will not only create a network of people you can rely on for support but also provide you with tips to assist you in various stages of the process.

Recommendations from existing barndo owners may save you a lot of time in narrowing down everything from the best place to find supplies to the best team to use. They will also be able to provide information on their experiences with permits and local tax laws. Be sure to ask them what they would have done differently.

Find the Money. Budgeting and financing go hand in hand. To get to the most workable budget, you might have to revise your first plan a whole bunch of times. Fix your credit score, if necessary, pay off as much debt as possible and cut costs wherever you can. This will provide you with more workable capital. When you approach lenders, be open to moving away from the more conventional options. Farm creditors and mortgage banks are great places to approach.

Pole or Steel. Another major consideration centers around whether you should opt for barn poles or steel structures. While this really is a matter of choice, we have to emphasize that a steel structure has considerably more advantages than a barn pole. These pros include everything from durability to general safety during storms. Don't forget that pole barns need to be specially treated for such things as wood rot and termites.

Assess DIY Options. One of the easiest ways to reduce costs and create more funds available in your budget is to do some of the work yourself. There are many tasks around the job site that you can do yourself. Some of these include painting, flooring and even drywalling if you have the know-how. Discuss your budget and potential DIY options with your general contractor. Be sure to do the DIY jobs when they must be done to not hold up the rest of the process.

Do Your Own Land Prep. Doing your own land prep can cut costs and speed up the building process. Land prep can be as simple as removing a bunch of trees and vegetation to require some serious excavation. Essentially, the more you can do yourself, the quicker the process can start after you receive permits.

Gather the Perfect Team. It's very unlikely that you're going to build your very first barndo by yourself. Not unless you plan to drive yourself crazy. This means it's of utmost importance to find the perfect team of contractors. Generally, you should only focus on finding the perfect general contractor. They will usually bring the right people for the job with them.

Plan the Work, Work the Plan. Decide if you want to create a custom build or opt for a kit. Keeping in mind that kits are often cheaper and easier to construct. They also come in so many different sizes and shapes that it's easy to find the perfect one. If your budget allows, consider stylish additions such as enclosed or wrap-around porches, outdoor entertainment areas and even a pool.

Strive to Be Energy Efficient. One of the top ways to ensure that your barndo dream doesn't cost more than it should in the long term is by opting for energy-efficient applications. Solar panels, skylights and energy-efficient appliances are only a few options to consider.

Permits First. Part of your initial survey of finding the dream location must include identifying the permit and zoning processes. Be sure to follow the specified regulations for your county and state to avoid unnecessary delays and penalties. Speak to your general contractor to assist you with this process. Be sure to keep copies of all the documents completed, submitted and received to assist with any future queries. Remember that work can only start when all the permits have been received.

Take the Leap. If you've already started your barndo process, we urge you to keep going. We hope that our tips and recommendations will help you take the next step to create your dream home.

There's no denying it. Building a barndo comes with many hiccups. There will be days when you'll question your sanity and then there'll be days that make you wonder why you didn't do this sooner! The open space and potential of a dual-purpose home in an area away from the rat race are well worth it. And lastly...

Pro Tip: *Savor every moment of your barndo journey by taking a ton of photos before, during and after the building process. Include photos of moving day and everyone's new spaces. Use these photos to create a photo memory wall in a communal space. It's a great way to capture the journey from start to finish. Not only will it be a great conversation starter, but it will be a daily reminder to you dear barndo dreamer, that dreams do come true!*

A final note from us. Our barndominium journey has been both difficult and incredible at the same time. Despite all the challenges we faced, we wouldn't exchange the experience. In addition to creating a spacious and unique home, we also have a wonderful space for our business. Furthermore, adding features such as skylights, under-floor heating and water-saving plumbing has made a considerable difference to our monthly energy bill. (And, honestly, who wouldn't love that?) As avid bakers, we must tell you that deciding to create a huge kitchen space was by far one of the top choices in our barndo-building experience. A large outdoor entertainment area combined with a stylish garden makes entertaining family and friends a breeze! The additional space has made our barndo a dream come true. Everyone in the Cohen clan wishes you much success with your barndo-build!

Enjoy Your Barndominium—After All, You Deserve It!

A Note From the Author

As the book comes to a close, we sincerely hope that you enjoyed the read. We hope this book has simplified the process and thoroughly inspired you to stop waiting and make your dream barndo a reality. Moreover, I would like to personally thank you for taking the time to read our book. If you found this book to be helpful, we would like to ask you to please leave a nice review along with some of your favorite parts from the book. We wish you the best in your journey and again, thank you!

References

A Guide on the Importance of a Barndominium Architect. (2022 May 4) ZP Architects & Engineers, www.zparcheng.com/blog/barndominium-architect#:~:text=There%20is%20one%20 key%20 reason. Accessed 3 Nov. 2022.

Barndominium Exterior Inspiration and Ideas. (2022) Clayton Constructionus, claytonconstructionus.com/barndominium-exterior-inspiration-and-ideas/. Accessed 3 Nov. 2022.

Broughman, Rachel. (2021, March 20) *What to Know about Barndominiums.* Family Handyman www.familyhandyman.com/article/what-in-the-world-is-a-barndominium/#:~:text=via%20 Metal%20 Building%20 Homes. Accessed 30 Oct. 2022.

Steel, Maverick. (2021 October 4) *What Aggregates the Price of a Barndominium Steel Kit.* Mavericksteelbuildings.com, mavericksteelbuildings.com/steel-barndominium-kit-prices-what-do-they-mean/. Accessed 30 Oct. 2022.

Chalmers, Ashley. (2022, October 3) *What to Know Before Building a Barndominium.* The Spruce www.thespruce.com/what-to-know-before-building-a-barndominium-5213835. Accessed 30 Oct. 2022.

Durrani, Ana. *The Barndominium Dilemma: Is It Better to Build One from Scratch or Refurbish a Barn?* (2022, August 3) Real Estate News & Insights | Realtor.com®, www.realtor.com/advice/home-improvement/build-a-barndominium-from-scratch-or-refurbish-a-barn/. Accessed 30 Oct. 2022.

Gillman, Todd. (2022) *Two Story Barndominiums: Prices, Floor Plans, Advantages.* Innovative Building Materials, innovativebuildingmaterials.com/design-inspiration/two-story-barndominium/. Accessed 30

How Much Does It Cost to Finish out a Barndominium? (n.a.) Outdooroo www.outdooroo.com/cost-to-finish-out-a-barndominium/. Accessed 30 Oct. 2022.

How to Build a Barndominium: A Complete Guide to Building Your Barndo - Barnardos. (2022) Barndos. barndos.com/how-to-build-a-barndominium/#How_to_Build_a_Barndomini um_Step_by_Step_Guide. Accessed 3 Nov. 2022. Oct. 2022.

Khan, Mohsin. (2022 March 29) *How to Increase Barndominium Energy Efficiency - Construction How.* Constructionhow.com constructionhow.com/how-to-increase-barndominium-energy-efficiency/. Accessed 30 Oct. 2022.

Kit Home & Barndominium Construction : Choosing a Contractor. (2020 October 21) Absoluterv.com, www.absoluterv.com/kit-homes-and-cabins/hiring-a-contractor/. Accessed 3 Nov. 2022.

McMinva, Mikayla. (2021 August 17), *How Long Does It Take to Build a Barndominium?* Metal Solutions, metalsolutionstx.com/barndominium-timeline/. Accessed 7 Nov. 2022.

O'Connor, Michael. (2022 February 9) *Building a Barndominium on a Budget: 8 Unique Tips to Consider.* Barndominium Life.com www.barndominiumlife.com/building-a-barndominium-on-a-budget/. Accessed 3 Nov. 2022.

O'Connor, Michael. (2021 April 26) *Top 10 Cheapest States to Build a Barndominium.* Barndominium Life.com www.barndominiumlife.com/cheapest-states-to-build-a-barndominium/#:~:text=Idaho%20is%20one%20of%20the. Accessed 30 Oct. 2022.

Olson, Sarah Asp. *7 Pros and Cons of Being Your Own General Contractor.* (2019 February 9) Rethink Rural.raydient places.com, rethinkrural.raydientplaces.com/blog/7-pros-and-cons-of-being-your-own-general-contractor. Accessed 3 Nov. 2022.

Rein, Tamara. (2022 September 26) *What Types of Windows Are Suitable for a Barndominium?* Prudential Cal, www.prudentialcal.com/what-types-of-windows-are-suitable-for-a-barndominium/. Accessed 3 Nov. 2022.

Scott, Aaron. (2022 January 7) *What Is Included with a Barndominium Kit?* Buildmax House Plans, buildmax.com/what-is-included-with-a-barndominium-kit/#:~:text=The%20energy%20efficiency%20and%20the. Accessed 30 Oct. 2022.

The Beginner's Guide to Barndominium Homes. (2021 October 20) Extra Space Storage, www.extraspace.com/blog/moving/buying-selling-renting/your-complete-guide-to-barndominiums/#:~:text=How%20Much%20Does%20a%20 Barndominium%20 Cost%3F. Accessed 30 Oct. 2022.

Made in the USA
Monee, IL
20 January 2024

52119434R00097